Between

Children as a Zone of Peace
Peace

Varindra Tarzie Vittachi

Much love to
Madeline,
Mum.
xxxx
Christmas '9?

Hodder & Stoughton
LONDON SYDNEY AUCKLAND

British Library Cataloguing in Publication Data

Vittachi, Tarzie
  Between the Guns: Children as a Zone of
  Peace
  I. Title
  363.706

  ISBN 0-340-60231-/

Published by Hodder and Stoughton,
a division of Hodder and Stoughton Ltd,
Mill Road, Dunton Green, Sevenoaks, Kent TN13 2YA
Editorial Office: 47 Bedford Square, London WC1B 3DP

Photoset by SX Composing Ltd, Rayleigh, Essex
Printed in Great Britain by Cox and Wyman, Reading,
Berks.

Contents

Acknowledgements

The author and publishers would like to thank the following for their kind permission to reproduce the quotations contained in this book:

Routledge & Kegan Paul for permission to quote from Simone Weil's *The Need for Roots*, translated from the French by A F Wills and originally published in France by Gallimard

Doubleday for permission to quote from *Children of War* by Roger Rosenblatt

Basil Davidson and James Currey Publishers for permission to quote from *The Black Man's Burden*

Jessica Kingsley Publishers for permission to quote from *Reaching Children in War: Sudan Uganda and Mozambique* by Cole P Dodge and Magne Raundalen (1991)

Hal Leonard Publishing Corporation for permission to quote lyrics from *South Pacific* by Rodgers and Hammerstein

TRO Essex Music Ltd for permission to quote lyrics by Woody Guthrie © 1956 & 1958 Ludlow Music Inc, USA. All rights reserved.

Foreword

Varindra Tarzie Vittachi, whom I am proud to know simply as "Tarzie", in no small measure changed my life. It is largely due to his extraordinary powers of persuasion, to his compassion and his energising optimism that I became a Goodwill Ambassador for Unicef in 1987. Through my work as a film maker, I have, over the years, been granted the privilege of meeting many remarkable men and women but few as patently good, honest and true as this noble Sri Lankan whose love of children – all children, everywhere – has shaped his life. I am honoured indeed that he has asked me to put my name to the foreword of this book.

In the western world children are invisible. We don't see them where we spend most of our time – at our workplaces, where we meet to have a drink and talk with friends, where we debate the events of the day, or in the places we go to be entertained. We see them in bed or preparing to go to school, and possibly at the weekends if they have no other commitments and we ourselves are available to share what we rather affectedly call "quality" time with them. It is not so in Africa, Asia or Latin America. Children seem to be with their parents most of the time. The family is an economic and social unit comprising not just the parents and children but the families of their aunts and uncles, elder brothers and sisters who continue to live in the same community, the extended family.

You would like to think that this arrangement is "natural" and therefore blissful. It might well be but for the terrible impact of sheer poverty on the lives of those families. Many children stay home or drop out of school at 8 or 9 because they are income earners for the family unit, like the young cotton pickers in Egypt, or because they serve as energy substitutes used for fetching firewood and water in homes where there is no prospect of electricity or running water. Many children are often sick from diarrhoea, chronic malnutrition, infection through lack of rudimentary hygiene. Some 13 million die each year from preventable diseases. And when the family income ceases because the father is out of work it is easy to imagine how the litany of childrens' suffering becomes longer and more inhuman.

For example, there are children whose conditions are not in the eye of the world's conscience because they are no longer of interest to the broadcast and print press. They were the subject of yesterday's news before the guns were silenced and they are no longer newsworthy. They have become invisible. These are the 15 million refugee children who are euphemistically called "unaccompanied minors". They have managed to limp across a border and find shelter in camps set by the High Commissioner for Refugees, Unicef, the World Food Programme, Oxfam, Save the Children organisations and a score of religious aid societies. There are millions more who have not been able to cross a border but have had to flee their homes and have become separated from their parents. They are not called refugees because they must cross a border to qualify for attention from the High Commissioner for

Refugees and are thereby deprived of the scant benefits of a refugee camp. We could meet them on the streets of the exploding cities of the Third World scratching a living off the streets.

The most threatened are the children of civil war, the most vicious arena of human cruelty to other humans. These wars are largely the result of the breakdown of Nation States which were formed in the late 19th century or early this century by compelling ancient linguistic, ethnic and religious nationalisms to co-exist within the same territorial boundary, often an artificial boundary drawn on a map by a departing colonial government. When the imperial age passed, the new rulers of independent countries claimed these borders as an integral part of their inheritance and continued the imperial policy of central rule and management of the lives of people belonging to these sub-nationalisms. It is the centrifugal revolt against this that we are now experiencing in large and small territories like the former Soviet Union, the former Yugoslavia, India, Sri Lanka and other once-colonised Nation States.

The suffering of course falls on children of both sides. This is a terrible reality as we have seen in El Salvador, Uganda, in the Horn of Africa, the former Yugoslavia and in the Sudan. Yet it is also the point of possible change as Tarzie Vittachi describes so compellingly in *Between the Guns*.

When, through his advocacy, I was appointed Unicef Ambassador, Jim Grant, its Executive Director, was excited by the possibility of turning crisis into opportunity. He has a long three-generational intimacy with China and it was natural for him to think in those sagacious ways. He and his associates persuaded both sides in the civil wars in El Salvador, Uganda and the Sudan that it was good politics to protect children from preventable disease and from their guns, and bad politics not to. When Dubrovnik was under siege, he persuaded Belgrade to let him take a ship in to evacuate the children of that beautiful city. Corridors of peace for children were built through the air, through the sea, through the land and the jungles. Most remarkably, on the very day that General Omar Hassan Al Bashir overthrew Al Mahdi, the President of the Sudan, Grant was in Al Bashir's office pleading successfully that the Corridors of Peace for Children, permitted by his predecessor, should be continued. Even more remarkably, Al Bashir agreed to let Jim Grant and his aides fly over government-held land and use the roads to negotiate with John Garang and other rebel leaders in the South.

National sovereignty was, and is, important to all the Heads of State in these countries wrecked by civil war. But, evidently, there was some deeper consideration that was even more important: their concern for the wellbeing of children. May we even hope that this acceptance of the concept of children as a zone of peace, even as the reason for peace, will prove to be the motivating force of a new human ethic which will lead us to the end of war, a goal we have not been able to achieve through many millennia of civilization?

Richard Attenborough

1
A Dream of Children

This is the story of one man's dream of a world safe for children. Seeing the planet riddled by terrorism, civil wars and subnationalist conflicts (there were more than seventy "small" wars raging at that time, 1984), Nils Thedin wanted children everywhere to be regarded as a "conflict-free zone".* He asked Unicef, the international agency for children, to take the initiative in giving substance to his dream. Having headed Rada Barnen, the Swedish Save the Children organisation, for many years, he knew that there were many non-governmental organisations and private individuals all over the world who would respond to such a lead. He had some authority in assigning this task to Unicef, for he was the principal delegate from his country to Unicef's Executive Board, and he had been a formidable force in Unicef almost since its inception in 1946. When he made his proposal to Unicef, he was already ailing from a terminal illness and he died a few years later.

But the dream did not die with him. Jim Grant, the head of Unicef, heard Nils Thedin's plea for children in

---

* His actual words were: "Unicef should awaken an awareness, all over the world, of the special status of children. In the document on Unicef's external relations as well as in the medium-term plan, reference was made to the possibility of promoting children as a conflict-free zone in human relations. It should be Unicef's ambition to turn that ideal into a reality."

trouble in his inner ear which resonated to such a grand human idea. He implored his staff to think of ways and means to put living flesh and bone on the idea and set his own mind on seizing the first opportunity to bring Thedin's dream into reality. It came two years later when he used his gifts of indefatigability, his deft political footwork, and his skills of persuasion to build the first conflict-free zone for children. It was in fact a time-zone, not a geographical space, and was established in El Salvador where the government of President Napoleón Duarte had been fighting a formidable rebel movement for several years.

Now, less than a decade later, the concept of zones of peace for the innocent non-combatants of wars seems to be spreading through the embattled world like a benign infection. Governments, non-governmental organisations, religious hierarchies and United Nations agencies have now adopted the language of "Corridors of Peace" and even the methods used. These corridors feature particularly in civil wars, in which former peaceful neighbours attack one another even more ferociously than in international wars, where the enemy is a faceless, nameless, unknown mass of human beings engaged in a quarrel between two or more nation states. Cross-border war is impersonal while civil war is a personal fight which seems to stir the most intense depths of primordial bestiality in the human mind-set. (To interject a light note here, at the risk of being charged with what Freud called "situational irresponsibility": Oscar Levant, the pianist and actor, was asked whether he thought he was capable of murder. "Murder? Murder?" mused Levant. "Hmmm, friends perhaps, not strangers!")

Elated though we may be that Thedin's dream is becoming a reality, we must take a moment to realise that it is only a small beginning in the eternal human quest for a world free of war, a globe-wide conflict-free zone for children. As long as there are sovereign borders protected by the rival armament of armies in conflict, military cultures will thrive, and wars which uproot, cripple and kill millions of children will continue. And as long as the rulers of these nation states, protected by the military, insist on concentrating all decision-making power, whether political or economic, in their own hands, they will ignore the peripheries of society where the minorities live and dream of giving reality to their own identities, and civil war is on the cards.

The nation state as a benevolent construct, in which all minorities are expected to know their place and their limitations in the access to political and economic power, and to accept the magnanimity and the sense of fair play of the ruling majority as a serious and unbreakable pledge, has already proved in a score of countries to be a tragic hoax. The future of the children of minority groups is constantly at risk from the racist demagoguery which is a sure-fire election winner. That is the reason for the willingness of minorities to make superhuman efforts, go to any lengths, put themselves to any cost, make whatever sacrifice it takes, to protect their future – that is, their children – from these dangers. To an anonymous poet who has no country we owe this memorable line: "National boundaries are wounds on the skin of Mother Earth." He was writing about catastrophic threats to the environment. The poem goes on to warn us all that as long as artificial human divisions such as economic blocs and nation states exist, we will continue to live by divisive values: black-white, north-south, my patriotism versus your patriotism, when the only patriotism appropriate is what Pérez de Cuellar, the former Secretary

General of the United Nations, called "Earth Patriotism".

Sensing that all life on Earth is in grave danger, thousands of people of every class, caste, creed and ethnic group have begun to realise that we are all members of one race and that we must join hands if we are to undo the damage we have done to the environment. We also "know" the truth, however uninformed we might be of the facts, that we alone – not any other living thing on this Earth – have brought about these dangers. And we have realised, dimly at first, more clearly later, that unless we act together as one people, peaceably and reasonably, mutually reinforcing our efforts, our children and our grandchildren will be denied the gift of life and the opportunity of growing to their full height in body, mind and spirit.

Children are the only personified symbols of terrestrial immortality we know, the one way that the meaning of the lives we have lived can be given a continuity while our material bodies return to the earth. We have constructed "other" lives for our spirits "elsewhere" – beyond the outreach of our minds – from our hopes, from our imaginings, from out of our enormous depths of gullibility, our intuitive gropings for faith, and from our intellectual reluctance to accept the notion that our lives have had no meaning, no substantial relationship with time and space and to accept the bleak conclusion that it was nothing more than an ephemeral experience between the parentheses of birth and death. Many of us struggle with such doubts all our days, in our religious faiths and in our workaday philosophies, and never seem to be able to resolve them even when the priest is at our dying bedsides. That is why for most of us, the last reaching-out is towards our children.

Biologists may find that this universal "love" for children is a piece of primordial information written into our genetic code to enable us to survive as a species, and to flow with the evolutionary stream. They may not. However that might be, we humans have often behaved as though this is one of the things we are sure of. And we will continue to do so unless we change the values which have powered the behaviour that has brought us and all living things to this critical fork in the road. Shall we thoughtlessly carry on as before, warring against one another and destroying the biosphere, or shall we change our ways?

At Unicef in New York, the internal debate continued. Jim Grant, always thrusting to give life to promising ideas to benefit children, pressed us to "programme" Nils Thedin's idea of "children as a Zone of Peace". In common language this meant "make it work".

There isn't much time. The litany of children's sufferings had lengthened in the previous two decades. Children were being mobilised as mine-sweepers on the battlefronts of the Iran-Iraq war. Poor little devils, they were told that to die in what their mullahs had decided was a "Holy War", qualified them for immediate translation to Paradise. (The children of the mullahs and their friends were denied this boon of immortality by being sent to schools in London, France and other safe havens.) Children were being trained by guerrilla forces – in Ethiopia, the Sudan, Honduras, Nicaragua, Mozambique, the Philippines, India and Sri Lanka – to use rifles for some cause many of them could barely understand. In Latin America, children were being abandoned in tens of thousands because their fathers had abandoned their mothers, possibly because of their chronic joblessness (a state in which people begin to feel worthless, and worthless people cannot be called to assume responsibilities).

Or the children themselves had abandoned their homes and taken to the streets to fend for themselves as parking assistants, "runners" for the small shopkeeper, prostitutes, pimps, drug-pushers or whatever occupation would bring them a peso for survival. *"Mama calle,"* replied a Bogotá street-boy of about eight when I asked him why he had left his mother. The street was his adopted mother. The street fed him and kept him alive. No one had accurate figures for the total number of street kids but the guesses ranged from forty million to seventy million in Latin America alone.

Unicef's responses to these problems were "programmed" as far as its bag of contributions allowed. But since the problems were mostly rooted in gross poverty and abysmal underdevelopment, no single agency of the United Nations system had the means to deal adequately with most of them, unless the quantity of aid were raised far beyond what the international conscience of the time would bear. Jim Grant decided to take the advocacy route. Unicef's people in 120 countries became children's advocates with their governments. In his words, Unicef became "a handful of people with a handful of money," urgently pressing government leaders to take better care of their children. It did not matter whether the government was "democratic" or "authoritarian". Children are above and beyond politics and ideologies. He went to General Babangida who had just toppled the democratic civilian government of Nigeria, and to President Belisario Betancur Cuartas of Colombia, who headed a democratically-elected government, and persuaded both of them that it was good politics to vaccinate all the children in their countries against the preventable diseases which were maiming and killing them; and bad politics not to. Grant had the political sense to know that Unicef needed enormous political skill to maintain its ethic of being a "non-political" instrument of action for children. But the most intractable of all the tragedies remained: the children of war.

One afternoon in 1984, opportunity knocked. A historic meeting between President Napoleón Duarte of El Salvador, Jim Grant, the Secretary General of the United Nations, Pérez de Cuellar, and his senior undersecretary-generals, led to the genesis of the ringing phrase, "Days of Tranquillity for the sake of children". And that gave rise to the Corridors of Peace and Zones of Tranquillity which were later installed in Africa and the Middle East where large numbers of children were caught in the crossfire of warring forces.

The experience of negotiating those Zones or Corridors of Peace and managing the system of supplying food, medicine, vaccines and basic necessities through them evenhandedly, the constant vigilance and high morale needed when agreements are violated by one side or the other and the increasingly widespread acceptance of the concept of Zones or Corridors of Peace to protect children, is the theme of this book. It is a new and difficult idea. It has often to be negotiated between belligerents when their warlike passions are at boiling point, rather than when both sides are tired and ready to resort to mediation.

And it is a conscious and deliberate intrusion against the long-held principle of sovereignty, demarcated by territorial boundaries which are jealously protected, though many of them were not set by topographical features but by mere squiggles on a map drawn by some colonial administrator. The world-wide phenomenon of the breakdown of once monolithic nation states into cultural-linguistic homogeneities, is generally regarded with trepidation by those who have gained power through statism and have a vested interest in maintaining the nation-state concept as being a historically, if not divinely, sanctified principle of effective governance.

Such are the political and psychological considerations which have stood in the way of rapidly extending the Zones or Corridors of Peace for humanitarian purposes. Could Zones of Peace for children become a universal phenomenon enshrining man's humanity to man as a sacral principle even in the midst of war and violence? Could Nils Thedin's imaginative notion that children everywhere should be recognised as a Zone of Peace one day become the thin end of a wedge between war and peace? Let us look for an answer to that question in the experience of Unicef in the past ten years in a Yeatsian world in which the centre cannot hold and the beast has been slouching towards the holiest place of all – the child's cradle.

Nils Thedin's idea that children were a Zone of Peace was not something he conjured out of a sentimental imagination. It has a long history and a human context which gives the notion of "children as a conflict-free zone" a respectable past and therefore possibly a viable future. The moral basis for Henri Dunant's success in establishing the International Red Cross as set out in his *Un Souvenir de Solferino* (1862), his memorial to the wounded and sick victims of the bloody battle of Solferino, gave literary expression to that ancient but often latent human trait of caring for the helpless. And though the Red Cross was almost exclusively concerned with battlefield victims, its moral foundation was the same as that which led Nils Thedin to speak for the non-belligerent innocents victimized by war.

8

A Dream of Children

Towards the end of World War One, Eglantyne Jebb, a leader of the suffragette movement and a founder of the British Save the Children Fund, had gone with a group of associates to the ragged frontlines to provide what is now being called "humanitarian assistance" to needy children on both sides of the conflict. She was charged in the British courts with the crime of having given "aid and succour to the enemy". From there on, the story takes many different forms in which some details differ. The version that my sense of drama prefers is succinct and memorable: she arrived at the courthouse in a blaze of newspaper publicity, escorted by George Bernard Shaw who, the reporters thought, would be her advocate and character witness. She did not need one. The charge was read to her: "Are you guilty or not guilty of having given aid and succour to the enemy?" Her response was: "My lord, I have no enemies below the age of eleven." Naturally, Miss Jebb was acquitted.

I say "naturally" because many ancient writings originating in China, India, Indonesia, West Asia, Africa, Europe and Latin America, and interwoven into the ethical matrix of all human faiths, recognise what Nils Thedin refers to as the "special status" of children. Poets, along the long line from Valmiki and Shakespeare to Tagore and Neruda, had inner ears to hear the sound of children weeping. In "Cry of the Children", Robert Browning asked directly:

Do ye hear the children weeping, O my brothers,
Ere the sorrow comes with years?

He commented:

They are weeping in the playtime of the others,

9

In the country of the free . . . And lips say,
"God be pitiful", who never said, "God be praised."

All of us know that somewhere within our nature is a
Zone of Peace for children. This is probably why many of
us – journalists who write today's history on the run, and
have experienced the way people everywhere behave,
whether they are being beasts or angels, or just boring
nine to five wage-earners – believe that the day on which
the United States irretrievably turned away from the
Vietnam War was the day on which that stunning photograph of a naked Vietnamese girl, a child of six or seven,
running up a road crying out to be held and protected
from napalm and the killer guns, was published on the
television screens and newspapers. On that day, the core
of humanity within even the warmakers was touched. We
have all been taught war and to admire warlike values
such as the will to win, and the killer instinct in our competitive games. But there is a Corridor of Peace in our
inner being, always, for a child to run through for
protection.

At the same time that the horrors of Vietnam were
occurring, the principle of regarding children as a Zone of
Peace was being applied in Africa where one of the
earliest examples of ethnic centrifugalism drew world
attention and empathy. Biafra, where the Ibo predomi-
nated, made a strong bid for independence from central
control from Lagos, the capital of the Federal Republic of
Nigeria, where the government was predominantly
Hausa, Yoruba and Fulani. The Ibo, as large a minority
as the Yoruba, had established a secessionist state in
1967 under the leadership of Lieutenant Colonel Ojukwu,
with its first capital set up at Enugu. Between May 1967
and January 1970, the Nigerian government enforced
rigorous economic sanctions and bombed the population

and cities of Biafra mercilessly. Ojukwu was compelled to move his capital three times, to Aba, Umuahia and finally to Owerri. More than one million lives are estimated to have been lost in military action. The breakaway Republic of Biafra lost its oil reserves and was soon experiencing acute shortages of food, essential drugs and other basic needs. The children, of course, were the main victims of deprivation.

In the midst of all this violence, Unicef, evoking its mandate as the world's agent and advocate for children, moved a small task force into Biafra to receive emergency supplies from its cornucopian storehouse in Copenhagen and to distribute it to the battered cities. Unicef's emblem – mother and child girdled by the protective fronds of the United Nations symbol – became as distinctively and admiringly recognised as it had been in Europe in its first years when it carried out its massive rescue of children whose lives had been blasted by bombs and shell-fire. What is most notable is the deftness of the diplomacy which made this humanitarian intrusion into the "sovereign state" of Nigeria possible. The government of Nigeria, like every other member-nation of the United Nations, insisted on the inviolability of its hard won "sovereignty". What this meant was that anything that happened within its "sovereign" borders which had been charted by colonial officers managing the retreat of imperialism, was the exclusive business of the government of the Federal Republic of Nigeria. If the Ibo who had dared to challenge the authority of their central government were suffering from the military actions intended to maintain the "unity" and "integrity" of Nigeria, they had to take their medicine, which was bitter enough to be a deterrent against any other secessionist ambitions. And it was no one's business but that of the sovereign government of Nigeria.

But when it came to children, a higher law than sovereign rights and territorial imperatives prevailed. Children had a supervening right to protection from the consequences of governmental or anti-governmental forces struggling to attain and retain power. This was the basic principle which persuaded the government of Nigeria not to declare *persona non grata* the Unicef staff whose office was in Lagos and to "allow" Unicef to carry out a parallel humanitarian action in Biafra. This humane principle of giving importance to aiding the helpless and vulnerable non-belligerents caught in war also shielded non-governmental institutions such as the International Red Cross, Oxfam and the Christian Aid groups while they were operating in Biafra without imperilling their work elsewhere in the Federation.

A shift in values in human relations is becoming evident, from an almost exclusive concentration on the "rights" of a dominant majority towards a recognition of obligations towards a minority, which includes access to security, health care, schools and all the benefits a government affords to its nationals. Rights have to be desperately negotiated between disparate groups, a process which always ends, not in a genuine consensus or convergence of purpose, but in compromise which appeases many minds but leaves no one's heart satisfied with the outcome. A recent case is the Convention on the Rights of the Child which was picked at, comma by comma, for ten years before it was sent to the General Assembly of the United Nations for approval. In some important aspects, the compromise achieved weakened some of the gains for children which had already been made and which were enshrined in previous conventions achieved by the International Red Cross, the International Labour Organisation and Unesco. Approaching a need such as protecting children from the standpoint of moral obligation, on the contrary, causes relatively little debate except when it gets embroiled in the stale and soulless rigidities of ideological syllogisms.

Simone Weil makes the point lucidly in her transforming classic, *The Need for Roots*:

> It makes nonsense to say that men have, on the one hand, rights, and on the other hand, obligations. Such words only express differences in point of view. The actual relationship between the two is as between object and subject. A man considered in isolation only has duties, amongst which are duties to himself. He, in turn, has rights when seen from the point of view of other men, who recognise that they have obligations towards him. A man left alone in the universe would have no rights whatever, but he would have obligations.

In the spiritual ethos to which I myself subscribe, everything has an inner and an outer dimension. Rights are the outer dimension of human relationships, obligations the inner. Rights are the coarse physical expression of a finer inner sense which binds human beings in the web of social relations. It is in this insubstantial inner space that we will find the true source of our feeling of obligatedness towards children. And when we are conscious of the quality of that inner source, we will be able to give it an outer reality by recognising its existence in others, and building a zone of compassion, with their agreement. However rough and bellicose their reputations and their outer characters might be, they are not likely to be totally devoid of that one trait which distinguishes man from ape.

This is the spirit behind Nils Thedin's ideal of awakening everyone to regard children as a conflict-free zone. And it is what led Unicef to make a beginning in turning "that ideal into reality," as Thedin implored, by inducing the government and the rebel forces engaged in a long and bitter civil war in El Salvador to pause, to take their fingers off the trigger for a few days to enable Unicef and the International Red Cross to do some benign shooting of a different kind – immunising their children against diphtheria, whooping cough, tetanus, measles, TB and polio, the six "vaccinable" diseases which destroy little children. The vaccination needle was the instrument used to breach the solid wall of sovereign statism and clear the rubble of civil war for a Zone of Peace for children.

2
El Salvador:
Days of Tranquillity

At Unicef, Jim Grant had set his mind on achieving immunisation of the world's children by the year 1990. As far back as 1974, the World Health Assembly of Health Ministers from 120 countries had resolved unanimously to attain that target so that the nearly five million children who were dying each year from vaccine-preventable diseases would be saved.

In 1984, Unicef set about it with great gusto. Jim Grant believed that nothing but a clear and indisputable demonstration that universal immunisation by 1990 (naturally labelled UCI 1990 – Universal Child Immunisation by 1990) was "do-able", would make the target achievable despite the pressing deadline. Indeed, like a newsroom which produces its best work under pressure, Unicef as a whole rolled up its sleeves and got down to it (although of course there were the usual percentage of paper-clip counting bureaucrats who preferred their business-as-usual routine). Colombia was chosen as the first campaign venue. It had several advantages: relative proximity to Unicef headquarters in New York: high levels of literacy among both men and women; a good transport network; a comparatively large base of already immunised children – around thirty per cent; an effective media system, both print and broadcast; and, most valuable of all, a highly cultivated and empathetic head of state, President Belisario Betancur Cuartas.

An accelerated participatory process which Jim Grant labelled "Social Mobilisation" was launched in Colombia. He first convinced Betancur that protecting Colombian children from preventable diseases was the most precious gift that a president could give to his people. This was in keeping with the principle enunciated in the mid-fifties by Sir Arthur Lewis, the celebrated West Indian economist, that there could be no development without "political will". This idea had been avidly adopted by the international community and by academia, but its practitioners had interpreted political will to connote the will of the government, and especially its head. Grant too believed that the will of the head of government was essential, but he took the principle one step farther toward sustainable effectiveness. He knew that the political will at the top had to be reinforced by the political will of the people, informed and supported by the media; the religious orders and the non-governmental organisations; women's organisations; youth groups; popular musicians, writers and artists; the country's educators; every organised group including the armed forces and the police services; the trade unions, and indeed everyone who could spread the word if it was to "go to scale" nation-wide and be maintained at an effective level. Within a few months, many of these groups were mobilised to become actors in a development drama which galvanised and involved the entire nation.

On the day the campaign was launched, the President himself sat in the operations room in Bogotá, monitoring the process at work through television, radio and telephone links with the governorate. It took on the excitement and pace of a national election campaign. The "returns" of children immunised were reported by monitors around the country to the ops room. Late that afternoon, a dramatic event was reported from a remote mountain province. A truck carrying vaccines had broken down on a narrow mountain road, blocking all road access to the area. The Governor sent an SOS to the ops room. It was treated like a national emergency. The military provided a plane. Unicef packed it with another stock of vaccines and ancillary equipment. By the time all this was ready, night was falling in the mountains. The Governor reported that there were no runway lights on the airstrip. But that problem was solved when the police chief broadcast an appeal on car radios requesting motorists to drive over to the airfield and beam their headlights on to the runway. The vaccines were delivered and the day was saved.

Social mobilisation proved itself not only as an effective strategy but also as a permanent boon to the country. The active involvement of so many sectors of society had reminded everyone who participated that successful development was not something that was passively dependent on foreign aid combined with state action, but a common popular effort in which many kinds of people played active roles in their own life-drama of survival, growth and sharing.

This was the example soon adopted and followed by Turkey, Sri Lanka and Nigeria, in that order, and by every country in which Unicef was working. In Sri Lanka, Farid Rahman, the Unicef representative, created tremendous popular interest in the immunisation campaign by persuading the austere Board of Cricket to let him paint the campaign slogan on the holy ground on which a Test Match between Australia and Sri Lanka was being played. There was nothing more sacred than saving children's lives, it seemed, not even the sacred game of cricket. And Colombia's success in rallying so many varied groups of its people to the call for children, and Unicef's ability to spread that word around the world, were what excited President Napoleón Duarte of El Salvador to ask for a similar exercise to be carried out in his country. That was the beginning of the series of Zones or Corridors of Peace which have since been built in Africa and the Middle East.

El Salvador was a politically thorny country for a major Unicef initiative. It was one of those countries which was referred to in the oblique language used in the lobbies of the United Nations as an "unpopular country". Why "un-popular"? Because the government of El Salvador was widely regarded as being a United States client and its military forces were believed to be supplied by Washing-ton. Unpopular among whom? In the Third World as a whole, and certainly among the Third World delegates to the Unicef Board. The Europeans, more particularly the Scandinavians who have a powerful voice at Unicef board meetings, almost unanimously considered El Salvador with much the same disdain as they did Honduras: as a piece of rather tatty real-estate that Washington con-sidered as its political backyard and which the US wanted to keep clean from what was regarded as the deadly pollutant of "Godless Communism". Jim Grant was a Stevensonian Democrat, with an international reputation for his sensitiveness to the needs and cultures of the developing world. But he was an American. He had to tread warily if he was to lead Unicef into a big operation in El Salvador. He had been appointed as head of Unicef on the recommendation of the Carter administration. Now Ronald Reagan was in the White House, with Jeane Kirkpatrick heading the UN Mission, and the Heritage Foundation was fanning the acrid fumes of American hostility towards Third World countries and the United Nations. Those were the days when many Americans had a field day throwing stones at the glass house on Turtle Bay. Mayor Edward Koch, with two masterfully ill-chosen words, denounced the United Nations as "that cesspool".

Grant's dilemma was how to intervene in the guerrilla-held areas of El Salvador without drawing the wrath of those Americans who thought that the rebels were heathen dupes of what President Reagan called the "Evil Empire" and how to increase the rate of immunisation on the government side without provoking Europeans and the developing countries on his Board into tearing him apart for getting Unicef involved in "an American problem". The only way was to immunise children everywhere in the country and take a moral stand on the principle which the Unicef Board had reiterated many times over its forty-year history: children are above and beyond politics. Maurice Pate, Unicef's founding Director, used to ask people: "Have you ever looked into the eyes of a child and discovered any politics there?" Grant's vindication was going to be: children *are* a Zone of Peace.

But the very idea of Unicef attempting a country-wide immunisation campaign while a bloody civil war was raging and overnight people were becoming "disappeared" (one of those curious verbal innovations of modern civilisation), never to be found, seemed to many to be quixotism at its zaniest. There is nothing more

sinful to the bureaucratic mind than a bureaucracy
taking a risk. And this was a big one. But even the most
courageous risk-taker must secure the key elements of
the venture which tend to become unmoored under pressure of rapidly changing circumstance. In the case of El
Salvador, Unicef had to be sure about the durability of
President Duarte's will to go through with the idea of
calling his army to heel while the vaccination campaign
was being carried out in the whole country, and also
about the reliability of the agreements being negotiated
between Archbishop Arturo Rivera Damas and the guerrilla leaders who were constantly on the move.

A visit to President Duarte was needed. In October
1984, Jim Grant went to El Salvador. His first appointment was breakfast – what the Americans call "a seven
o'clock" – with the US Ambassador to El Salvador. This
was Tom Pickering, an old friend who not long after
earned international renown for his no-nonsense ways as
the US Permanent Delegate to the United Nations
during the Gulf War crisis, when he was instrumental in
welding a disparate group of nations into the coalition
which confronted Saddam Hussein.

Duarte asked Grant if he would help El Salvador to increase its immunisation rates for children as Unicef had
done recently in Colombia where a participatory national
campaign had involved the government, the Catholic
Church, the media, the military, police and non-governmental organisations. Parish priests in Colombia
distributed pamphlets with the stunning message: "Thou
shalt not kill, nor shalt thou let a child die from a preventable disease." *El Tiempo*, the big national newspaper, featured a new cartoon character on page one of a
boy born the week before the campaign who was the first
to be symbolically vaccinated by the President himself.

20

The campaign succeeded in raising immunisation rates from some thirty per cent to around seventy per cent.

Grant agreed to President Duarte's proposal, provided Unicef would be allowed to immunise children in the entire country. Of course no president can possible concede that he has no access to any part of his country. He agreed, leaving it to Grant's diplomatic skills to carry it through. Jim Grant went to Rome to secure the help of the Pope to reach the rebel areas of El Salvador. The Vatican wrote seeking the cooperation of Archbishop Arturo Rivera Damas in El Salvador.

Pickering suggested that Grant should request Duarte to appeal publicly for a nation-wide ceasefire to guarantee the safety of the mothers and children coming to the vaccination centres, and also of the vaccinating teams. What was needed was not just a ceasefire of three days a month for the coverage but a few days of peace before the campaign started so that people would feel safe to leave their homes and travel some distance with their children. This meant arranging a series of ceasefires and maintaining the level of interest among the parents over a period of three months, during which the combatants would be fighting a stop-go war.

At lunch that day with Duarte and the military commander, Grant proposed the ceasefire plan. He recalls the tense silence which followed. Duarte turned to his senior general and asked: "How long do you think I would remain as President if I asked for a ceasefire as Mr Grant suggests?" And the general, hardly hesitating, answered sardonically: "Oh, about three days." Duarte explained to Grant that his calling for a ceasefire would "give too much status to the rebels".

Such are the nuances of diplomatic language in war and peace. Words are intended not only to communicate and discommunicate but also to offer status to or debase someone. A head of government cannot even suggest a ceasefire when embroiled in war, international or domestic, without implying that his side was losing and wanted either to sue for peace or gain time to reinforce his army. A president proposing a ceasefire would immediately send a signal of weakness to the rebels ranged against him as well as to his allies and critics abroad.

Grant countered: "What if we arrange for the rebels to agree unilaterally not to shoot on those days? Would you also be willing to agree unilaterally not to shoot?" Two unilaterals making an unlinked bilateral agreement! Why not? It happens all the time in family quarrels. President Duarte replied, "Oh yes," and agreed to order his troops to observe the days of *tranquillidad* during the vaccination campaign. This was how the term Days of Tranquillity originated and inspired related terms such as Zones of Tranquillity, Corridors of Tranquillity and Corridors of Peace. These terms came to be used in Africa and the Middle East with a sort of natural ease which suggested that those words and the message they carried had always been in the vocabulary of all nations. It was the genesis of a new, officially recognised ethic which comes into effect when human relations are at their worst, when people are at war with themselves. It indicated a time of tranquillity to be interposed between people engaged in a killing exercise, who dig into their human nature and find a quiet place deep down there to respond to the quiet day outside on the battlefront for the purpose of taking care of children. The Zone of Peace, in Nils Thedin's words, "children as a conflict-free zone", was not a geographical place or delimited space which could be pointed out on a map. It was an essence to be discovered or, rather, rediscovered in the tranquil core of the human heart.

The campaign was set to begin on December 17, 1984 as a Christmas gift for the children of El Salvador. Only two months to go and many complex logistical and political problems still had to be resolved. The logistics alone were a nightmare. The Ministry of Health had attempted an immunisation campaign earlier, using trained volunteers from the Salvadorean Red Cross. But this was a failure. The volunteers explained that they "could not find the target population". No wonder. There were thousands of displaced families with no fixed abodes on both sides of the conflict. Even the notion of "sides", with its suggestion of recognisable demarcations, did not accord with the reality on the ground. The fighting moved rapidly from place to place. The guerrilla forces would take over an area and after a short period move on elsewhere without leaving behind a garrison to hold it down; then the official army would come in for a while, moving on again soon after to another area which the guerrillas had taken over. This dizzying process left the people shaken and impoverished, and intensely charged with distrust of any protestations of objective altruism by anyone. Volunteers who had been directed towards a set of villages and small towns often found that the road which had been marked "clear" today was blocked by guerrilla pickets tomorrow. These encounters increased the guerrillas' suspicion of "officialdom" with which the volunteers were associated, even though their ostensible purpose was seen to be "good for the people".

On their own part, the volunteers feared these confrontations with the guerrillas and were reluctant to expose themselves to danger. And to make things worse, there was a persistent rumour that the guerrillas, whose supplies had recently been topped up, would be launching a heightened military campaign in the months leading

23

up to December, the month scheduled for the immunisation campaign.

On the bright side was the fact that the President's resolution held. His promise of cooperation for a genuine effort to raise the level of complete immunisation from the unacceptably low level of some three per cent to something approaching national scale was held to firmly and his attitude had percolated down the military hierarchy. Suggestions were rejected that the date should be moved forward to overcome the logistical difficulties that were being pointed up by government officials. They were instructed to put solutions in place rather than try to postpone their responses to the need. Pleas that the rainy season was coming and that the peasants would be migrating with their families in the late months of the year in search of employment, fell on deaf ears. The immunisation campaign was "go". The Ministry of Health heeded Unicef's determination and the army provided the transport to carry health personnel engaged in the campaign. The government genuinely regarded the campaign as a national undertaking, important for all Salvadoreans. The politics of civil war, however, do not follow the textbook formulae of diplomacy. There is no easy "leverage" to apply. There is no real-estate to be traded for the gain of one side or the other. There is no sententious appeal such as "patriotism" accompanied by the flag to flaunt. Salvadoreans are all *compadres*. They bleed alike about most things that concern them. And in El Salvador, they were all Catholics. There are no "tactics" and "strategies" to be employed by the peacemaker, especially a peacemaker entering the scene for the limited purpose of establishing a zone of peace to immunise children. There is only trust. And trust has to have been earned over a long period of intimate association, by the style and effectiveness of performance.

Between September and December, the political agenda had to be reviewed. Negotiations had to be concluded between the government – the Ministries of Defence and Health – the army commanders; the guerrilla groups; the International Red Cross in Geneva; the Salvadorean Red Cross; the Pan-American Health Organization which had been working on the Expanded Programme of Immunisation for many years; and with the Catholic Church which undertook all the contacts with the rebels along with the military, as the chief mediator assisting Unicef in the cause of children.

Archbishop Arturo Rivera Damas and his energetic associate, Bishop Gregorio Rosa Chavez, represented the one organisation which had the trust of most El Salvadoreans. The Church had a crucial role in the country in the defence of human rights and the needs of the poor. The guerrillas too were Catholics, and respected (some of them very deeply) the place of the Church in their family lives. They were keen that the children in areas under their control should be immunised and some of them actually trained themselves to do the vaccinating when the time came.

The Archbishop insisted that he would accept the role of mediator on two conditions: that the immunisation campaign should not become, nor be seen to be, a political stratagem of the government, and that it should cover the entire country, not just the government-held areas. Under these conditions, the Church would use its good offices to smooth out the wrinkles that would inevitably appear during the campaign, obtain the safe-conduct passes for the medical and technical teams who needed to cross war-zone boundaries. Archbishop Rivera Damas obtained these agreements through secret meetings with guerrilla leaders, some of whom were operating from as

far away as Mexico. He and his network of priests undertook to monitor continuously the successes and de-
ficiencies in the process and to correct any shortcomings
while they were happening, and most important, to lend
the enormous moral authority of the Church to advocate
to parents the need to bring their children in for vaccination. In every church, homilies were preached on each
Sunday before and after a Day of Tranquillity to reinforce
the message that children should not die from preventable diseases when health measures were at hand.

One of the first things to be done was to find partners
for the enterprise. The head of the Pan-American Health
Organization, Dr Caryle Guerra de Macedo, was concerned, as Jim Grant had been when he talked with the
President, that more children were dying in El Salvador
from immunisable diseases than people killed in the war,
so Dr Macedo was willing to chance it. For him, the three
per cent rate of immunisation in El Salvador was professionally quite insupportable. The International Red
Cross offered ready cooperation. The two men were both
ready to persuade their colleagues in El Salvador to coop-
erate with the Ministry of Health in the training and
deployment of vaccinators and to see that the "cold chain"
– simply, the ice-boxes in which the vaccines had to be
stored – were in place and in good order. Unicef was to
supply the needles, sterilising equipment and the vaccines from its great storehouse in Copenhagen, and also
the coordination needed for the job through its small
national office in El Salvador. Pickering had advised
Grant to tell the President about an earlier idea of bringing vaccines, equipment and personnel from Nicaragua
into the rebel areas. This was intended as a diplomatic
nudge to persuade Duarte to see that his military forces
would be cooperative in letting Ministry of Health and

Red Cross personnel in Unicef vehicles cross the scrappy, unmarked frontlines into discrete fighting zones. It would also have been, in a sense, "internationalising" the Zone of Peace which was being constructed, with the attendant risk of upsetting the Reagan administration's fiercest hawks by showing the Sandinistas in a humanitarian light.

In the event, this approach proved to be unnecessary. With the cooperation of the Minister of Health, the Unicef office in the capital was able to manage the supply line from the capital. Largely because of the extraordinary support of the Catholic hierarchy, headed by the Archbishop whose humanitarian heart had been strengthened by the Vatican's positive letter, the rebel-held areas were brought on track for the campaign. The Archbishop began to play his essential mediatory role between Unicef and the guerrillas. It was not easy. The guerrilla leaders in the field were hard to find because by nature, they were quick-silver mobile and when they were found, they were profoundly distrustful that the government would keep its word. They pooh-poohed the whole idea at first, denouncing it as nothing more than a propaganda ploy to win popular sympathy for Duarte's men who were facing an election. They feared that the government army would use any lull in the fighting to discover the concentrations of guerrillas, and suspected that they would violate any ceasefire period in deed and spirit. In the event, the few cracks in the truce were indeed caused by army personnel.

Hernan Jaramillo Hoyos, Unicef's coordinator in the field, recorded in his personal diary:

The Army detained the immunisation teams on

several occasions, despite their having proper documentation and identification. Five guerrilla commanders requested the vaccinators not to enter [because] the army was bombing the area . . . On the eve of the second immunisation day I was informed over my walkie-talkie that the army was bombarding some areas in an open breach of the agreements. We had to rush to the Bishop's and the Health Minister's houses to insist on bringing this bombing to a halt.

These breaches of the truce, however, were rare and are only noteworthy because in most of the country the military as well as the guerrillas honoured the agreement to cease fire.

The Salvadorean media featured the story of the campaign as important national news. Reporters and photographers who had been thwarted for many years by not being able to go into the rapidly changing conflict areas, and had therefore been constrained to publish handouts and hearsay, took advantage of the days of *tranquillidad* to produce authentic copy and pictures from the scene of action. Some of the pictures were models of "human interest" but two were outstanding: a woman guerrilla, carrying her rifle and military equipment on her back, vaccinating a child; a soldier using the foresight of his gun to pry open the crown cork of a Coke bottle for a thirsty mother who had trudged far to bring her child to a vaccination post.

Foreign correspondents had also suffered from the same frustrations, since most of them were based in the capital and unless, like a few intrepid individuals, they could gain entry via Nicaragua, they were unable to visit the guerrilla areas. Now they availed themselves of the lull in the fighting to visit areas in the country they had never before seen. Unfortunately, with the exception of the international wire services (whose reporters must file copy every day and are relatively less inhibited by the need to avoid rejection by the professional idiosyncrasies and news-value judgments of particular copy-tasters), the international Press paid very little notice to the extraordinary human story that was unfolding in El Salvador. The British papers published a Reuters story, and the *Miami Herald*, an Associated Press despatch from El Salvador. The *New York Times* reporter James Le Moynes ignored the first Day of Tranquillity, but after some nudging from New York, motivated by Jim Grant's intercession with Abe Rosenthal, the Executive Editor and an old friend from their time together in India, the second Day was reported, winning space as a single column top. In the Press, as in government, alas, it is often who you know rather than what you know that makes a story. In this instance, Rosenthal, who was a tough Executive Editor and spinily suspicious of any "influence", was professionally right to override the foreign news desk. The willingness of long-embattled enemies in a violent civil war to stop shooting bullets long enough for vaccinators to do a different sort of shooting, a benevolent needle in their bottoms, was quite definitely a story according to the most stringent and pernickety journalistic standards.

And so Days of Tranquillity came to international attention as an idea, and "children as a Zone of Peace" became a reality, in this case a time-zone rather than a space on a map. The dream in the mind of Nils Thedin took its first step to becoming a reality on the hot, rugged battlefields of El Salvador.

The impressive rise in the number of El Salvadorean children immunised in the first set of Days of Tranquillity declined soon after the last round of the campaign, thus giving detractors of the campaign approach justification for bleak "I told you so" smiles. But many benefits remained durable. More children than ever before were protected against immunisable diseases. Their parents, who had been mentally and physically involved in the Days of Tranquillity by bringing in their children for vaccination, had now become active participants in a "development" effort for their children.

They had experienced the possibility that, however poor they were, they could make a positive contribution to protecting their children from what previously had been regarded as ineluctable and tragic fate. They had become, in effect, the ultimate units of a health "infrastructure". As the activist groups working on improving the environment have learned, once men and women participate actively in a single positive action to improve their own conditions, there is no going back to the old habitual ways. They would repeatedly return for more of the new experience, which gave them an exhilarating sense of taking part in a community drama. And indeed they did, coming back with their new infants and providing an example to their neighbours to seek, even demand, the benefits of immunisation by taking their children to the Days of Tranquillity programmes which went on regularly in El Salvador until the end of the civil war six years later, when more than eighty per cent coverage had been attained. In the process, the Pan American Health Organization was able to introduce other interventions such as nutrition education, family planning advice and facilities under its own rubric of "Health: a Bridge for Peace".

Another permanent benefit was that the Salvadorean experience of Days of Tranquillity gave heart as well as experiential lessons of value to other efforts to protect children caught in the violent turmoil of civil wars in Uganda, Mozambique, Somalia, the Sudan, Ethiopia, Liberia, Angola, the Lebanon, Sri Lanka, the Philippines and, not long after, on the European Continent in Yugoslavia. Children, at last, were becoming denizens of conflict-free zones cut out for them in the perilous centre of civil war.

3

Corridors of Peace Through Air, Land and Sea

The Beast Unleashed

All the Zones or Corridors of Peace listed at the end of chapter two were international interventions in civil wars. Each of them was triggered by a different "original cause" or action by one side or the other. Those causes and the actions which ensued were often rooted in ethnic, religious, linguistic or economic class differences among the people living within the same borders – by their own wish or by the imperatives of history, geography, economics or the prevailing ideologies – some of them the products of fifty years of Cold War – which had impinged on their lives. But all of them had a common cause: the wish of individuals and groups, big and small, to attain and retain political and economic power in the name of "causes", ennobled by such grand designations as "patriotism", "nationhood", "cultural integrity", "liberty", "equality", "ethnic purity", "mother tongue", and a myriad similar triumphs of the sloganeer's art.

Some of these causes were objectively justifiable in terms of the human need to prevent the erosion or forceful suppression of deeply-held values and time-tested linguistic links which have bonded people together for millennia. Some, however long they have been touted as being innately human, ("patriotism", for instance, which is usually taken to mean the idealising of the nation state and, even more often, of the coterie in power attained by election or force) are spurious. They are often mere inventions designed to vindicate the manufacture, sale and use of deadly weapons and to promote a military culture. And all of these causes, with increasing ferocity, lead to the slaughter of the innocents – non-combatant men and women and their children.

Ay, there's the rub. One of the principal motives of insurgency is to create civil disorder so that the ruling authority, against which armed dissidence is ultimately directed, has to deploy a great deal of its time and resources in trying to restore and maintain order, while it is embattled with the rebels who are described by the state-controlled or state-owned Press and broadcast media in various pejorative terms, such as "militants", "extremists", "terrorists", "anti-national elements" (anti-national meaning anti-state) and, of course, "Communists". Public disorder is most easily brought about by attacks on civilian populations. In the process of creating disorder and restoring order, thousands of people lose their homes, their crops, their livelihoods and their lives. The terrorism of the rebels is counter-matched by state terrorism. "Bodies floating down rivers" was a common story in Indonesia where in 1965-6 the army killed off some 350,000 people to suppress what was perceived as a Communist threat of insurgency. And in Sri Lanka, uncounted numbers of villagers in areas which the Southern Sinhalese rebels operated from were despatched by bullet and bayonet and thrown in rivers by the army to "teach a lesson" to those who survived the onslaught.

The beast in the human mind is unchained and let loose in civil conflicts where there are no rules of war to temper its bloodlust. As soon as a civil war breaks out, a government usually resorts to martial law or emergency regulations which effectively suspend the Constitution and all the regulations which limit the deployment and use of armed power. The other side makes up its own rules as the conflict spreads, the only effective rule being the insistence on success measured by the degree of chaos and mayhem its agents have caused. Observing so many internal conflicts in my own country and around the globe in the past forty years, I have often wondered whether our vaunted human culture has only put a superficial veneer on the animal within the human being. Whenever that thought begins to trouble me I remind myself that below that bestial layer there is a human being whose true nature is compassion, tolerance and considerateness.

But that redemptive thought is being constantly disavowed by experiences of observed reality. Cole Dodge and Magne Raundalen tell this terrifying story of Carlotta, a schoolgirl in Mozambique:

> We were all singing and dancing and then suddenly the bandits came. They said they were from the other village and started dancing too. Suddenly they turned off the music and we tried to leave when they started shooting. I ran away and hid in an old house. While I was hiding the bandits discovered me. They forced me to go with them and when we passed through my village, they put fire to my grandmother's house, but it was empty. They stole

food and kidnapped a lady. We were so many and they killed so many that day. They asked a woman to carry a bag of salt. She carried it halfway but then she said, "I am so tired."

"Oh, you are so tired?" the bandits said.

"Yes, I'm so tired," she replied wearily.

"OK, you will rest for ever," they said.

Then they killed that woman and she died right in front of us.

But all efforts to wedge a corridor through Mozambique were frustrated mainly by the fact that the insurgency was largely motivated by intrusion by the South African government which had adopted a policy of destabilising its leftish neighbours, particularly Angola and Mozambique. Nevertheless the Zones of Peace for children initiative seemed unquenchable even in conflicts which were so hopelessly ravelled, and the brutality so intense that anything thought of as a humanitarian intervention seemed pointless, even impossible.

Uganda: The First Air Corridor

When, after eight years of terror, Idi Amin was driven into exile in 1979 by the Ugandan National Liberation Army strongly supported by Tanzanian forces sent in by Julius Nyerere, three short-lived governments tried unsuccessfully to put some democratic order into a country which had become accustomed to strong one-man rule, but had never reconciled itself to it. National elections were held in December 1980 and Milton Obote, who had been ousted by Idi Amin more than a decade before, became President again. There were widespread complaints at home and abroad that the polls had been rigged. There was so much unhappiness among the people that a few months after Obote's installation, it encouraged Yoweri Museveni to lead a small band of twenty-six men into the scrublands to form the core of the National Resistance Army which set itself the task of waging guerrilla war against the government's forces, the Ugandan National Liberation Army.

Three years of civil war ensued, with Museveni's movement gaining ground as well as thousands of recruits, many of them adolescents and children. The guerrilla movement also had support from the Buganda tribesmen in the areas in which it operated and from Ugandan exiles and political sympathisers from neighbouring countries. In 1983 Obote launched a series of seek-and-destroy campaigns which took a massive toll of life in the Luwero Triangle, the centre of gravity of the dissident movement. Cole Dodge, the Unicef representative in Kampala, reported that some 200,000 people had been killed, 150,000 forced into camps run by the UNLA and 150,000 had become displaced persons, or refugees within their own country. "Thousands of homes were destroyed," Dodge wrote in *Reaching Children in War*. "Communities were dissolved and the fabric of social life in the Triangle [was] shredded. Families ran and hid in the bush to escape the atrocities ... Malnutrition and starvation escalated."

Museveni's resistance movement which had by now become a full-scale populist movement could not ignore the plight of the families of its supporters. Children were given basic self-defence training so that, according to the guerrilla leaders, they could defend themselves against

36

the seek-and-destroy missions of the government. Inevitably they became camp followers, gofers, and then were "adopted" into the movement. The use of child-soldiers by the Ugandan National Resistance Army drew considerable criticism. The BBC broadcast a vivid documentary entitled *Uganda: Children of Terror*. Museveni lost some sympathy abroad but not at home or in neighbouring Nairobi, for instance, where the child-soldiers were elevated in the hyperbole of the Press into "the Young Heroes".

It was in this atmosphere that Cole Dodge began to build the first Corridor of Peace in Africa. (For a full personal account see *Reaching Children in War* by Cole Dodge and Magne Raundalen, published by the Scandinavian Institute of African Studies.) His materials and tools were nothing but the Basic Agreement which Unicef always makes with governments, promising it "access to all needy children" and freedom to "assess the conditions and publish findings on children throughout the country"; the relevant Geneva conventions which empowered the Red Cross in Uganda to become partners in this enterprise; a deep belief in the reputation of Unicef as the world's agency and advocate for children and, most important, a large endowment of chutzpah. This was his armoury against men like Milton Obote and Brigadier Basilio ("Tito") Okello who had both seized power and ran the government with manic egos which brooked no dissent.

Cole Dodge possessed an acute sense of the value of massing public opinion behind Unicef programmes, not only for facilitating fund-raising but also for the purpose of letting the combatants in a civil war know that the world was watching. National borders were no longer impervious to the thrust of information and communication.

He also knew well the importance of joining hands with other groups – inter-governmental, bilateral and non-governmental agencies such as the International Red Cross and Médécins Sans Frontières (Doctors Without Borders) when he was about to implement a difficult plan like building a Corridor of Peace for children through one of the most hellish conflicts in recent memory. For a model he had only El Salvador's Days of Tranquillity. He drew three principal lessons from that experience of Unicef: the importance of going to the top and to hell with the prissiness of protocol; the value of linking up with the Red Cross and drawing from its rich fund of experience amassed through more than a century; and the necessity of persuading the media, which was deeply sceptical particularly during the Reagan years about anything that the United Nations did, that he had a good story to tell.

As in El Salvador, the vaccination needle was used as the point of entry for the Corridor. Dodge was able to persuade Uganda television to broadcast a six-part mini-series financed by the UN Development Programme entitled *Give Children a Chance*. The public was asked some pointed questions like, "Are you satisfied with Uganda today?" and "Do you want to leave your children with a better tomorrow?" – which sounded very much like, "When did you stop beating your wife?" But people across the country were now aware of their children's need of health measures. The programme showed them that more children were at risk from diseases preventable by immunisation than from the civil war itself. The information groundwork for the corridor was laid.

The question now was what kind of corridor? Road or air? Internal or external? A combination of road and air seemed the most appropriate. Dodge was pressed by colleagues to have the goods needed for children delivered from Nairobi or elsewhere across the Ugandan border where storage would be more secure and delivery more assured. He decided to play it straight: to go to Obote's government and to Museveni and obtain their agreement for the corridor. Negotiations with the government – with the Foreign Ministry, the Health Ministry, the Interior Ministry and the army chiefs – were carried out face-to-face. There were enormous bureaucratic hurdles to surmount, the most difficult being to get the Foreign Ministry to bend the regulations which insisted that every foreign national required a special permit every time to undertake even a short trip outside the immediate vicinity of the capital. Dodge, on his part, took the high ground that his mandate, as stated in the Basic Agreement between the government and Unicef, had granted unrestricted access to children in need. Eventually a compromise was arranged permitting travel by Unicef for the specific purposes for which the corridor was being established. The compromise protocol is a masterpiece of diplomatic cant: "We advise you not to go to the conflict zone because we cannot guarantee your safety but at the same time, we do not deny Unicef staff access to all parts of Uganda to serve the interest of needy children."

For the first time a corridor was cut through battle lines. In El Salvador, following the two unilateral agreements to cease fire while children were being immunised, parallel immunisation programmes were the order of the day. The conflict-free zone for children was a time-zone. Here, in Uganda, it was a geographical conflict-free zone which let personnel, drugs and equipment pass through from one side to the other.

The BBC, now an empathetic reporter of a good human story from Africa, carried the news that both sides in the civil war had allowed five different Unicef–Red Cross flights across the battle lines to immunise children. The news was repeated on state television and radio, the government claiming the kudos: "We have been encouraging Unicef to take supplies to the rebel areas; after all, we all have children and we are all Ugandans." The first peace flight took place on United Nations Day, October 24, 1986. There was some concern that the agreements made with the leaders would not be honoured at lower levels because of miscommunications. Dodge radioed the staff of the UN High Commission for Refugees in Fort Portal on the rebel side and requested confirmation that the NRA commander and the man responsible for guarding the airstrip had been instructed to expect the flight. They were. And so the Corridor of Peace was established in Uganda. The first air corridor. The first to cross battle lines. The first in Africa.

Cole Dodge had another item on his agenda: to persuade Museveni and his fellow guerrilla-leaders that inducting children into the guerrilla army was a regressive act. At a long meeting between Cole Dodge and Museveni in early 1986, approval for the Corridor of Peace and a more humane dispensation for the child-soldiers was agreed. Museveni thought that there had been "too much fuss" made about these child-soldiers. It had been a practice since pre-colonial times. Cole Dodge, in *Reaching Children in War*, presents both sides of the case on these soldier-children, an account which is refreshingly different from the familiar knee-jerk reactions of many advocates of children.

He then reports that there were two principal options for Museveni. The first was to keep the children in the army, and give them a formal education to supplement their military training so that they would fit into society when the war ended. This was a serious option because

40

many of the children had known no parental care since the war began; the rebel army, for which they worked in pre-teen years as gofers until later they learned to bear arms, had fed them, clothed them and sheltered them all their days. Indeed some of them had been informally "adopted" by soldiers who took direct responsibility for them as surrogate fathers. Besides, many of the children were loth to leave, preferring not to risk an unknown future, even if they could be reunited with their families, could they be found.

The other alternative was to place the children in civilian schools, under the responsibility of their surrogate army-fathers. They would be given a minimum primary education and a vocational skill. With this education behind them, they would have the option of an army career or of finding a civilian livelihood. In the meantime, efforts would be made to locate their surviving parents who would assume "normal" responsibility.

The advocates of the proposition that child-soldiers were an unredeemable abomination were concerned about their psychological prospects. Being raised in a military culture presented all sorts of grim possibilities. They were bound to carry the scars of violence etched into their minds during their impressionable years. There was the example of Idi Amin who carried into his early middle age the violent ways he had learned as a child-soldier to support this attitude. Revenge as a motive for living could become a common phenomenon among Ugandan children, as it had become in Northern Ireland and in the Middle East where children raised in a violent scenario assume that violence is the only acceptable way of living a purposeful life, and thus perpetuate the cycle of war. The seventeenth-century playwright and poet, Edward Young, had written:

41

Souls made of fire, children of the sun
With whom revenge is a virtue.

But Dodge, who himself detested the notion of using
children as soldiers, refers to a 1984-5 study he and his
colleagues made of 650 children in Kampala, Masaka and
Jinja where they found scant evidence of motives of vengeance in their minds. He sees this as encouraging but
does not assume on that basis that there is justification
for using children as soldiers, nor that the trauma of
violence is not damaging to most, if not all, children.

A great deal of study is being done on the impact of
military employment on children, particularly young
boys. But most of it ignores, or plays down, the social context in which the phenomenon of child-soldiers occurs.
This arises, I suspect, from the familiar assumption that
adults have a special moral exemption to behave badly –
for example, to drink themselves into a fighting frenzy or
into a dehumanising stupor; to use "bad" language; or to
practise violence and shoot one another in war to resolve
real or imagined disputes. But their young are required
by them to behave well at all times despite all the horrors
they experience around them at home, at school, in the
streets and on television. The adult proposition that there
are things worth killing for (often these "things" are bits
of real-estate called national borders) and causes such as
"flag" and "ways of life" or ideologies worth going to war
over – and their expectation that their children must
wait until they finish their "education" and reach chron-
ological adulthood to be allowed to join in such grown-up
pastimes – does not hold up in the minds of modern children, who grow old before their time.

Lebanon: The Impossible Peace Zone

The stock example of an impossible conflict-free zone for children was the Lebanon. Jim Grant and colleagues like Richard Reid, his Regional Director in the Middle East, André Roberfroid who managed the Beirut office, and Raymond Naimy, Unicef's intrepid and legendary "water carrier" who will long be identified with his *vis-à-vis* in the tarot pack, were told over and over again that the Lebanon, where a chaotic civil war had been getting more and more ugly over more than a decade, was one of those impossible places because no political solution was even remotely in sight. The very idea of trying to get children immunised under those circumstances was sheer lunacy. But men and women who are mad enough to take on the impossible, as long as its purpose accords with their zeal, are not easily dissuaded. Their quixoticism was vindicated by their success and also by an international pledge made later at the World Children's Summit in 1990 attended by more than seventy heads of state and government: "Resolution of a conflict need not be a prerequisite for measures explicitly to protect children and their families to ensure their continuing access to food, medical care and basic services, to deal with the trauma resulting from violence and hostilities." "Children as a Zone of Peace" was already being given international legitimacy.

Raymond Naimy, himself Lebanese, and possessing the negotiating skills of the best of his country's entrepreneurs, took all the time he needed to talk to each one of the warring factions. He said he wanted not just passive assent, nor even enthusiastic agreement. As he put it: "We wanted them to *own* the idea." His demand of them was not just one day of peace but several days – three at least – each month for three months for the children and their mothers to come to the vaccination posts, receive their complete array of recommended shots, and return home safely. They agreed. He was the water carrier, indeed the Water Department of Beirut. He had dug wells, installed pipelines, repaired broken ones, and organised mobile water-tanks to give the families of Beirut the gift of life at the worst of times when Israeli bombs had pounded Beirut to rubble. The people of Beirut believed that he could get Unicef to bring their children the gift of a future.

The detailed planning and negotiations with the power brokers in the 118 factions – the mullahs, priests, scouts, Red Crescent workers – were all done between May and October 1987 when the first round of the campaign began. By then there were vaccination posts set up all over the country, covering more than 2,000 villages. With so many participating actively to implement the purpose that they now felt they "owned", those Lebanese Days of Tranquillity took on the spirit and popular air of national festivals.

Suha Majdalani, a Lebanese Unicef information officer in Amman, went back home to observe the fun. She was stopped at a checkpoint. She just said "vaccination" and found to her joy and amazement that all the men at the guard post started singing the campaign song: "Vaccinate your child before it is too late. They are the hope; they are the future." They let her pass.*

Immunisation levels had risen dramatically. Vaccination rates for diphtheria, polio and tetanus had moved up from thirty or forty per cent to ninety-two per cent, and against measles to seventy-nine per cent. The protection of children and mothers at risk from tetanus infection had been carried to national scale. Thursdays were set as

---

* For a dramatic and detailed story of the Lebanese Days of Tranquillity see June Goodfield's *The Planned Miracle*, Cardinal Publishers, London, which was made into a BBC film.

regular vaccination days to sustain the impact of the drive. The lasting effects of the campaign were that public consciousness of the meaning and value of vaccination, already relatively high in "sophisticated" Lebanon, were raised to new levels, and parents now "owned" the right to protection of their children. Immunisation was now being demand-driven rather than supply-driven. The active involvement of the public and the galvanising of the health system had reinforced and extended the health infrastructure, even when operating under extremely difficult times of fear and disrupted services. And, as in the case of El Salvador and Uganda, the hopeful question arose: did the Days of Tranquillity in the Lebanon have any bearing on the eventual peace that came to this torn land after thirteen years of horror? And the answer, as before, was a cautious "maybe". How could that experience of respite from war *not* have had an effect on the habit of killing which develops in a society which has been living in a culture of attack and counter-attack, an eye for an eye and a tooth for a tooth, for so long? When the deep source of compassion for children is touched and stirred, is it possible for anyone to be indifferent or cynical about the human capacity to choose peace and reject war as a means of resolving human disputes?

And as before, there were numerous detractors, especially among organisations engaged in the same (or similar) business as Unicef. They resented the high profile which Unicef had once more acquired when some of them, like the officials in the Department of Public Health responsible for the Expanded Programme of Immunisation, the Save the Children Fund and the Lebanese Red Cross, had been beavering away at their work for years. They pooh-poohed the media stories as mere puffery organised by Unicef's information staff, and challenged the figures quoted for the low levels from which the numbers immunised had risen to new heights. They dismissed it all as a gigantic rodeo performance which "Jim Grant and his Cowboys" had brought to town. But the evidence that things had changed remarkably is undisputed by the parents who took their children for their shots through the Corridors of Peace where there was no need at all to flinch and cower at the sound of gunfire. Those times were short but, ah, they were sweet. Occasionally they still sing the vaccination song in the Lebanon: "Vaccinate your child before it is too late. They are the hope; they are the future."

Dubrovnik: The Hydrofoil Corridor

The siege of Dubrovnik in the autumn of 1991 brought Unicef back to Europe after forty-five years to help children. There was, at first, a natural reluctance to put its resources and time into a "developed" country because all Unicef's funds were meant to be spent on children's needs in the developing world. When millions of children were dying from malnutrition and disease in Somalia, how could Unicef concern itself with a European crisis which the rich nations could look after by themselves if they wanted to? Was it a concern for the children besieged in Dubrovnik and at grave risk from rockets and bombs, or was it the architectural and historical value of Dubrovnik as a city which impelled some European donors to put pressure on Unicef to build another Corridor of Peace between Belgrade and Croatia?

That was not the sort of question that Jim Grant would

dignify with an answer. Children in trouble was Unicef's business. And if in the process of running a peace corridor to rescue children, the destruction of the beautiful city of Dubrovnik were mitigated or even stopped, so much the better for all humankind. Unicef was already engaged in Somalia and was intending to intensify its work there, only waiting for the international community to provide the funds and the means of putting some orderly mechanisms in place to make a useful programme feasible. Besides, Unicef had become skilled at the art of getting the rich to pay for the poor in their own areas: witness Jim Grant's success in persuading the rich sheikhs of the oil countries to pay for Unicef's programmes in the Gulf. In the event, almost the entire bill for the peace corridor to Dubrovnik was paid by European countries in the form of drugs and medical equipment, food, clothing and, most important of all, the ships and trucks to carry them in and bring the children out to safe havens.

Jim Grant was concerned with much more intricate problems posed by any Unicef involvement in Yugoslavia: he needed the blessing of the European countries which contribute seventy per cent of Unicef's annual budget; he needed a formal request from the Croatian leaders, and a clear nod from Belgrade; he needed at least a "no objection" signal from the International Red Cross and the UN High Commission for Refugees to avoid possible turf problems, and he needed a green light from the Secretary General of the United Nations.

The European case for Unicef intervention was founded on the plain proposition that it would take Unicef's credibility and fame as an effective humanitarian agency to penetrate through to the toughened hearts of the new barons of Belgrade. The European Community, with all its power and intimate relationships with the former Yugoslavia, had failed to stop the bombing and destruction of one of Europe's loveliest cities. The European brief was carried to the United Nations Secretary General by Bernard Kouchner, France's Minister for Humanitarian Action. The Secretary General gave his blessing to "any humanitarian initiative" for the civilians in Yugoslavia, and Kouchner took Jim Grant's other conditions to Europe for a response. It came soon. President Mitterrand called a Press Conference to announce that he would make an appeal to Unicef to try to save as many children and their mothers from "the horrors of this war". This was followed the very next day by Roland Dumas, the French Foreign Minister, making a formal proposal to the EC to ask Unicef to intervene in Yugoslavia. There was no dissent and some enthusiastic support. The Italian Foreign Minister, Gianni de Michelis, immediately offered "all public assistance" to enable Unicef to carry out this new assignment. It turned out to be considerable.

The request from Croatia was soon in Grant's pocket. So were the positive signals from the International Red Cross and the High Commission for Refugees. The "no objection" sign from Belgrade was missing. It took a special visit to Belgrade by Bernard Kouchner, Margherita Boniver, the Italian Minister for Immigration, supported by Samir Basta, Unicef's chief at its European office in Geneva, and Stefan di Mistura, a young Italian who had served in the Sudan, to obtain a grudging "no objection" from Rear Admiral Popovic whose agreement was needed to move anything by sea in those dangerous Yugoslavian waters. This verbal nod was transposed to paper with a fax message from Samir Basta to di Mistura who had gone on to Rjieka to arrange a hydrofoil. In this document, "legitimised" by the Unicef letterhead, Basta laid out his "recollections" of the meeting with Popovic, and of his statement that he had no objections to Unicef going ahead with its water corridor for the relief of the children of Dubrovnik. That was Unicef's *laissez-passer*. It was all the owner of the vessel needed. Such are the ways of humanitarian diplomacy in these days when primitive human emotions and sophisticated communications rule the world.

The owner of the hydrofoil, the Atlas Company, generously offered the boat full-time, gratis, and for as long as Unicef needed it. His heart, according to a Unicef report, had been opened out that wide by di Mistura's canny suggestion that carrying the Unicef flag would make his boat safer from attack by the Federal Navy than anything else afloat, and that his company would be warmly remembered when tourist licences were being granted, beginning the day after the war stopped. Such are the ways of philanthropy.

Then the first major glitch appeared. Admiral Popovic, again by telephone, set down his own conditions: the vessel used had to be foreign; there would be no Press aboard; it should fly the Unicef flag; it should not stop *en route* except to refuel; it should move by daylight only and there would be no Croatians on it, except crewmen. Kouchner and de Michelis (both now out of office) made calls to their capitals about finding a vessel that would brave the risk of being attacked by the Yugoslavian Navy. It was not easy in such a short time. But Unicef staff are expert improvisers in tough situations. They "internationalised" the Atlas hydrofoil by the simple device of painting over its Croatian identification numbers and replacing them with the Unicef logo of parent and child. This brilliant naval manoeuvre was legitimised by ensuring that the owner informed Belgrade that the boat had been placed under Unicef's exclusive charge as of November 13, 1991. It was now an international vessel, under an international flag.

On the other side, two large Unicef flags were placed in "neutral" zones at the harbour and at the Argentina Hotel where the headquarters of the corridor was established. Kouchner and Boniver, appalled by the loss of life, the numbers wounded and the lack of milk or any other food for the children, had sent urgent appeals home for shipments to be speeded into Dubrovnik. At first, neither government wanted to get into a dog-fight with Belgrade, and expose their vessels to attacks by the Federal Navy. But when the "Unicef" hydrofoil wafted in safely and the European media reported it as one of the great instances of humanitarianism triumphing over the ugly side of humanity, the Italian and French governments decided to respond generously to the mercy call.

On November 19, Italy sent in a large vessel, the *San Marco*, with food, drugs and milk foods and safely evacuated 853 women, children and wounded civilians. The citizens of Dubrovnik experienced a palpable rise in their spirits, and the Press had another field day. Immediately, that old game of the human spirit, competitive philanthropy, began. France and Italy alone sent in thirteen ships which brought in more than 3,000 metric tonnes of basic necessities, including 1,200 tonnes of drinking water, and evacuated nearly 7,000 people, mostly children and their mothers. The corridor remained in operation till December 9, 1991 when, as di Mistura reported with some sardonic glee, the Federal Navy decided that, in the face of so much traffic on the sea lanes to Dubrovnik, it was absurd to claim any longer that the city was blockaded, and officially announced the lifting of the sea embargo.

The sea corridor and its widespread Press coverage also served to boost world outrage against the Belgrade authorities to such a pitch that a few days later, they stopped the bombing of Dubrovnik and ordered the obligatory enquiry to "round up the usual suspects".

Iraq: A Peace Caravan

The only instance of a Corridor of Peace in an international war, sometimes referred to as a "bubble of peace" because it was a one-off event rather than a process, was the intervention by a World Health Organisation–Unicef team led by Dr Ali Khogali of WHO and Richard Reid, Unicef's Regional Director in the Middle East. It delivered drugs, vaccines, oral rehydration packets, needles, syringes, nurses' kits and other basic mother and child health needs in a caravan of trucks that took the high road from Teheran to Baghdad through a time corridor arranged with the coalition command and the Baghdad authorities. Though this trek was a one-day event, the political skills and logistical intricacies which went into bringing it off successfully were extraordinarily adroit and complex.

Memory is a skittish human faculty and already – barely three years after – we have forgotten the political and military atmosphere in which the event took place. Saddam Hussein's military machine which had fought Iran for ten years, claiming victory at the end, was widely believed to be one of the most formidable fighting forces in the world. But such an army needs to feed on familiar food and needs to exercise its muscles. It was widely believed that Saddam would throw his army into another military adventure. Many thought he was planning an attack on Israel. That would certainly have been a case for the Book of Irony – American armament against American armament on both sides. As it happened, Saddam Hussein decided that he would first play an easier game: move his army into the borders of Kuwait abutting the Gulf and take over some of the oil-bearing real-estate which he had long claimed was Iraqi property. This idea did not seem to evoke hostility from his arms-supplier, the Americans. So he felt he could dare go the extra mile and take over the whole of Kuwait.

That, of course, was his mistake. The Americans would not let Saddam Hussein and his army control the oil supplies of the entire Gulf on which the US economy had become very dependent, particularly since the drop in the price of oil in the eighties. It was much less expensive, again, than bringing new domestic resources into production. The entire weight of the American political machine and the mass media was mobilised against Saddam Hussein. Within a week, this erstwhile friend and arms customer became an anti-democratic dictator who had crushed the small peaceful country of Kuwait. Indeed, he was a brown man's Hitler who had evil designs against not only Saudi Arabia and the oil-laden sheikhdoms of the Gulf on which the West was dependent, but also against Israel. Shades of the Holocaust were evoked and the media mumbled darkly about Hussein's capability of producing and using nuclear weapons within a year or, at most, two. With some extraordinary diplomatic dexterity President George Bush forged an impressive coalition of countries to turn the whole affair into a war between one man – Saddam Hussein – and the United Nations, much as Harry Truman had done forty years before in Korea when northern troops crossed the thirty-eighth parallel.

A thick wall of economic sanctions was erected in December 1990 to block all Iraqi commerce with the outside world. There was some hope that this embargo would bring Saddam "to his senses", as it was expressed, and that a shooting war, with all its attendant risks of escalating into a frenetic global affair, could be avoided. But the preparations for war brought their own momentum and President Bush was in no mood to halt them, if indeed that was possible. Soon the most formidable array of American forces since World War Two, supplemented by French, British and Saudi air and ground power, was entrenched in the Saudi desert by the middle of January 1991.

In the middle of January, the air forces of the coalition, commanded by General Norman Schwarzkopf, were bombing Iraq. They encountered some anti-aircraft action but, by and large, they flew in, dropped their bombs, fired their state-of-the-art missiles and returned to base with impunity. Saddam Hussein's Republican Guards, who had been credited with the victory over Iran and boosted by the Western media as "élite troops", cowered in their bunkers. There were no ground forces for them to engage if they came out, only the incessant rain of bombs.

Hussein had built up Baghdad into a modern city, where every amenity – water pumps and hospitals for instance – was powered by and reliant on the massive electronic grids which his engineers had constructed with American and European expertise. And this very modernity made the whole of Iraq, particularly its cities, extremely vulnerable to the interminable bombing. Blackouts were frequent in the hospitals. The children, as usual, took the brunt of it. The "cold chain" which protected the supplies of essential drugs and vaccines was destroyed. Milk foods which supplemented the diet of older children were unavailable except in the black market at exorbitant prices. Hospitals and clinics ran short of medicines and surgical supplies.

This was the scene in Iraq when its health and social services administrators appealed to the World Health Organisation and to Unicef for help. Unicef, according to its mandate and its ethos of responding to the needs of children in emergencies, was keen to move. Jim Grant had been born and brought up in China where his grandfather had been a missionary; his father was born there and had later established China's first public health school. China had imbued Grant with the tenet that a crisis always brought with it a beneficial opportunity, and he quickly perceived that this was an opportunity to extend the principle of "children as a conflict-free zone" (which had so far been applied only in civil war) to an international war. No amateur himself at dealing with international politics, he was aware of the enormous political and logistical difficulties which would hamper and even prevent a positive response to the *cri de coeur* from Iraq. He began the process of moving the barriers just enough to obtain agreement to get a train of trucks through a temporary humanitarian corridor into the city of Baghdad.

The politics of the United Nations was the first concern. He proposed a joint operation of WHO and Unicef. WHO was agreeable in principle but was concerned about being charged with flouting the sanctions. Grant was able to give reassurances. He knew that the key to the solution was in Washington. Using his expertise in manoeuvring through those bureaucratic minefields, and with the help of US Ambassador Tom Pickering and other friends in the State Department, he succeeded in persuading the White House that it would be politically advantageous for the coalition in general and the United States in particular to give their assent to a United Nations Mission which in partnership with WHO and Unicef, would operate a one-day Corridor of Peace in the war-zone of Iraq through which urgent health supplies for children would be carried. Similar negotiations with the Iraqi administration were carried out through the Iraqi delegation in New York, and in Baghdad by Unicef staff who had stayed on in Iraq despite the hail of bombs falling around them. The Secretary General's sparsely and carefully worded remit to the Mission was: "To deliver a shipment of emergency medical supplies to assist in the care of children and mothers, and to ascertain essential health needs".

The supplies were packed and ready for delivery at the Unicef storehouse in Copenhagen in the second week of February. The route chosen after much consultation was Teheran-Bakhtaran on the Iraqi border with Baghdad. It lay between the Iraqi forces bunkered in the north-east and right across the flight paths of the coalition bombers who were then flying 2,000 sorties every day. The coalition command received its orders to let the humanitarian caravan through and to give it protection from the air. Precision in timing was vital and every participating country's airmen had to be briefed on the operation. The trucks carrying the supplies had to be clearly marked so that they could be identified from far above the terrain.

The WHO–Unicef Mission which escorted the convoy consisted of: Dr Ali Khogali (WHO) and Richard Reid (Unicef) – co-leaders; Dr Abdullah Dirya (WHO); Dr El-Fateh El-Samani (Unicef); Dr Gianni Murzi (Unicef); Mr Raymond Naimy (Unicef); Dr Annette Vester (WHO).

At dawn on February 16, they set out from Bakhtaran

to cross the border into Iraq and on to Baghdad, passing Qasr-e-Shirin, Khanaqin, Al Miqdediyah and Baqubah. The journey was completed by late afternoon when the Mission was received by Iraqi Health Ministry officials in Baghdad. It had three days to accomplish its task. A brief extract from the Mission's report to the heads of WHO and Unicef tells the grim story:

> The mission found in Baghdad that normal life had come almost to a halt. The city's citizens now spend much of their time in family-support preoccupations, searching for food, trying to find water, and improvising cooking and heating amidst an acute shortage of all kinds of fuel. Baghdad has no public electricity, no telephones, no gasoline for civilian vehicles, and less than five per cent of its normal water supply. None of its water treatment plants is functioning. Toilets go unflushed, and unpumped raw sewage is backing up and overflowing in residential areas. Basic food items are scarce; rice and sugar are increasingly difficult to find. Most basic food items that are available are expensive. Meat is $36 per kilo – this in a society where $300 is the average monthly wage. Homes have no refrigeration for the preservation of food. Bottled gas for cooking and heating is so hard to come by that sales of it set off near-stampedes. The lack of heating fuel has left homes and public buildings so cold that the writers of this report have worn overcoats, sweaters, and scarves to all visits and meetings. Conditions in rural areas and other cities are said to be equally bad, and Basra is reported to be worse.

This was the basis of all the United Nation's humanitarian intervention in Iraq ever since. All supply lists were scrutinised in acute detail by American officials in Washington. Every dime spent on procurement had to be specially raised from sympathetic donors or paid for by Iraq, not charged to the standing budgets of the two agencies. Any suggestion that the sanctions were becoming porous or being applied leniently on Iraq in defeat was firmly rejected in word and manner. There was even some prevalent notion that the more the mothers and children of Iraq suffered, the more it was likely that the fathers would topple Saddam Hussein from his perch of power – a feat which the most powerful coalition ever forged to fight a single country had failed to accomplish with all its mighty armoury and secret agents. But, somehow, even this tough posture always yielded a little when it came directly to the life-needs of children and their mothers. The corridor to Iraq was the first in international conflicts. It will not be the last.

4
Sorrows of the Sudan

"Nothing good has ever come to the Nilotes from the outside," said Conradin Perner of the International Red Cross. He was trying to explain the suspicious attitudes of successive Sudanese governments and the rebel leaders, who were being persuaded by various segments of the international community to allow the safe passage of food, medicine and expatriate personnel, to relieve the sufferings of people whose lives had been shattered by the long struggle for identity and power in which Sudanese politicians had been embroiled for three decades. Nothing good for Sudan had come from the outside, because ever since the British had captured Khartoum for their stronghold on the Nile, the great waterway to the colonies they were building on the eastern edge of Africa, the Sudan was regarded as an imperial convenience, a spacious verandah between Egypt with its Suez Canal and southern Africa.

Little, if anything, was ploughed back into the soil. There was no prospecting for gold, diamonds, oil or other minerals. Christian missionaries did their prospecting for souls, particularly among the more wretched people of the South, where the promise of a better life elsewhere in another existence is more appealing because there is no hope in this. They made many converts. But colonial

Sudan consisted of small tribal villages and a few garrison towns. Very few macadamised roads were built and the only rail track lay east-west between Port Sudan on the Red Sea, Wadi Halfa on the Egyptian border and Nyala near the Chad border, and north-south between Khartoum and Roseires near the Ethiopian border.

When independence from the British came in 1956, this vast but poor country had no infrastructure in terms of transport, schools or adequate skills on which to build a nation state to enable the Sudanese to take their "place in the sun", as the political cant of the time expressed it. There were no electorates as they are conceived in Britain, India or elsewhere in the former Empire, but only tribes such as Fertit, Nuer, Mundari, Misiriya, Dinka (the largest group in the South) and Topasa, whose lifeways had been inherited from millennia of coping with the elements. They existed on a subsistence yield from the soil, from family farms producing food crops and from herding cattle. They formed frail but sufficient safety-nets against the unending harshness of their lives. Barter had enabled them to swap their small surpluses and there was a sense of cooperation, hospitality, tolerance of one another's ethnic or religious differences, and a tacit code of chivalry which protected women and children in the scuffles that inevitably took place between the tribes under survival pressures.

The northern areas are predominantly Muslim in religion and Arab in ethnic origin; the southern areas are predominantly Christian. But the traditional tolerance of the people has made it possible for small minorities differentiated by religion and ethnicity to coexist peaceably with the majority in both South and North. Indeed, in townships scattered around the country, which are prone to be less distinctively divided by race or religion, many

Arab–Black African marriages have taken place over time and their progeny have not suffered from social discrimination nor contemptuously been considered to be "half-breeds", as similarly situated children have been elsewhere in countries which consider themselves modern and civilised.

The Sudanese seem to have been able to escape a widespread human predilection for keeping their bloodlines "pure". In the late sixties, sharing a camp with the famous aviator Charles Lindbergh in the Mindanao mountains of the Philippines, where we were independently studying the habits of the T'Boli (or Tagabili) people, I remarked that he seemed to have become very fond of these "primitive" folk who still live in tree houses. I asked him about the wartime allegation that he was a racist of the Nazi mode. Lindbergh paused to consider my question, looked at my face, decided that I was not dirt-digging or being personally hostile, and replied: "I am not a racist. But I believe in race. The variety of races on Earth must be kept separate. That is what Nature intended."

As for the Sudan, the ethnic or religious differences between the tribal ethnic groups has not obscured their deep-rooted sense of being Sudanese. This spirit of oneness, or nationalism, leavened by history and reinforced by the fact of independence, has not yet disappeared in spite of the cruelty of the war within the nation state. The southern dissidents led by the Sudan People's Liberation Army/Movement, though being led by the Dinka tribe who are largely Christian, are fighting for autonomy and the guarantee of being able to maintain their cultural identity, but they have never demanded secession.[*]

---

[*] Recently, a faction of the SPLA, evidently despairing of a fair resolution of the civil war, has broken with tradition and said it wants to secede.

They consider themselves to be Sudanese through and through. And Lieutenant-General Omar Hassan Ahmed al-Bashir who toppled the elected Prime Minister in a *coup d'état* in mid-1989, and has fought the SPLA up and down the country ever since, refers to the SPLA and its corollary factions as "brothers".

"Government forces," he has said, "and the SPLA speak the same language. Both suffer directly from the war; they are comrades; some are friends with each other and can therefore talk easily to and understand each other."

The beginning of the corruption of these simple relationships came with the intrusion of another kind of colonialism. Cold War merchants were looking for customers around the world and found many poor countries in Africa susceptible to their salesmanship. The Horn of Africa was a good market into which they could put their competitive ideological wares and with them, the arms and ammunition to penetrate new areas and defend their gains. To counterpoise the presence and influence of the USSR in neighbouring Ethiopia led by President Mengistu, whose Communist forces, with Soviet help, had torn away the reins of power from the aged Emperor Haile Selassie, the Americans became Sudan's most munificent aid-giver. Much of this aid was for equipping and training the military forces. There was also the need, from the point of view of the United States, to provide its ally, Egypt, with a southern defence and also to show gratitude to Sudan for being the only African country besides Egypt to sign up in support of the Camp David Accords. American interests included also the possibility of US companies finding oil.

Underlying all these geopolitical considerations was the American fear of Islamic fundamentalism which they regarded as the new ideological disease they would have to fight. Already the long talons of Ayatollah Khomeini were scratching at the traditional mutual tolerance of the Sudanese and discovering that in high places tolerance had worn down to a thin veneer. In early 1982, President Nimeri, who had been in power on three occasions, went to the extent of imposing the *Sharia* – basic Islamic law – in all its Iranian ferocity at the instigation of the most influential and vocal Islamic group, the National Islamic Front. This heightened the fears of the southern Christians and also of the other less powerful and numerical Muslim sects such as the Khatmatiya and Ansar. This started the widespread supposition that the Sudanese civil war was a struggle for power between some twenty million Muslims and some six million Christians. Thus, a new ideological influence from abroad had come to Sudan to bedevil an already embattled situation.

There were, of course, other factors which interacted to exacerbate the hostilities between the two dominant religious groups. The army had played a predominant role in the independence phase of Sudanese history, and military leaders assumed, with some foundation, that they were the responsible proponents and defenders of Sudanese nationalism just as passionately as the Indonesian military leaders have done since their country was liberated from Dutch colonialism. Militarism as a way of life and an essential feature in the governance of people was interwoven into the social and political fabric. There was also the essential economic factor – the classic division of a few, who have more than enough wealth and landed property for themselves and their families; and the millions, who had nothing but a few head of cattle or a patch of scrubland to till and grow a few vegetables or some fruit, to sell in the bazaar for the cash to buy their foodstuffs such as salt, sugar and some of the staples they needed to supplement what they had scratched from the soil. Ownership of land was also skewed. The South has larger tracts of arable land and mineral resources than the politically powerful North where the capital is situated, but the money and tools needed to grow resources had not been allocated fairly or in sufficient quantities. And when the Christians in the South tried to bypass government budget-controllers and go direct to private benefactors from abroad such as World Vision International from the USA and the Lutheran Church societies in Scandinavia, they were smeared with charges of selling their country for the traditional mess of alien pottage. (The parallels between these realities and the historical events which led to the civil war in Sri Lanka between the majority Sinhalese and the minority Tamils are remarkable and instructive.)

These divisive elements inevitably led to civil war which, in its turn, had a devastating influence on food production and other survival resources. The safety-nets woven through the centuries frayed and finally broke down. Add to all this mountain of trouble the prolonged drought which has now become endemic in the whole region, being broken only by brief and occasional rainy spells, and the picture of mass misery becomes blacker still. And if those Job-like sufferings piled one on top of the other were not enough, the scant resources of the Sudan were further depleted when more than half a million refugees poured in from the civil war raging in Ethiopia. Tigreans and Eritreans shuffled across the border to benefit from the age-old spirit of hospitality of the Sudanese. And they obliged as best as they could.

The numbers of local refugees from their ancestral areas (who are referred to in the UN jargon as "displaced

persons" to distinguish them from refugees who have
crossed a national boundary, thus placing them outside
the ambit of the budgetary and programme responsibilities of the UN High Commission for Refugees) soared by
1985-6 to an estimated three million – about half the
population of the South. In the next two years, a possible
500,000 people died from war and famine. Larry Minear's
little book *Humanitarianism Under Siege* (a volume of
extremely instructive essays written by people who had
hands-on knowledge of these events and processes in the
Sudan, to which I owe much of the facts I have used here)
describes the tragic scene compellingly. To quote one
observation: "Half of these were children but only 6,000
were soldiers . . . the famine itself [was] one of the most
withering in modern times in terms of severity, scale and
duration."

Humanitarian intervention from outside was now
essential. The leaders of the factions were not on speaking terms, and their anger was too explosive for them to
reach out a brotherly hand to one another to prevent
more anguish for the victims of their conflict. Nils Thedin's prayer for regarding children as a Zone of Peace was
now more appropriate than ever as a motive force for a
peace maker to intercede.

As it happened, it was not Unicef which initiated the
corridor through which the survival supplies of these displaced hundreds of thousands of women and children
would be carried to them under safe-conduct promises
from both sides, but the Sudan Council of Churches, in
which both Protestants and Catholics are represented.
The Council alerted the United Nations agencies to the
critical state of the Sudanese people and, together with
Oxfam and other non-governmental activist groups,
undertook to negotiate a Zone of Tranquillity, or rather, a

Uganda-style Corridor of Peace. Late in 1986, working with Unicef which provided some of the supplies, the Council managed to persuade the Sudan People's Liberation Army to allow a convoy of Nile barges to carry food, medicines, vaccines and other supplies to people on both sides of the civil war. In the same year, World Vision International, collaborating with the Sudan Council of Churches and Sudanaid, the philanthropic arm of the Sudan Bishop's Conference, established a corridor through which they supplied 2,000 tons of food and other essential goods for the relief of Wau, a town held by government forces but besieged by the insurgents. Emboldened by this success, the World Food Programmed led by Winston Prattley, the Secretary General's Personal Representative, established a food corridor to supply Juba, Wau and Malakal and other townships besieged by one side or the other. The deliveries donated by eleven governments were made by Stefan di Mistura, then of the WFP. He later joined Unicef and, as we have seen, showed great courage and imagination in undertaking diplomacy and management of the Unicef corridor built to take in supplies for the children and mothers of Dubrovnik who were under siege from the government in Belgrade at the beginning of one of the most horrendous and barbaric civil wars in memory.

It was a tricky undertaking in the Sudan where neither the government nor the rebel leaders were comfortable with the corridor, code-named Operation Rainbow, which wove its way intricately through the fronts in the civil war. It was inevitable that misunderstandings and miscues would proliferate. And so they did. Government forces claimed that official permission had not been obtained for one particular relief flight or another and the SPLA threatened to shoot down supply planes heading for government-held towns. Both charged the UN with favouring the needs of people on the "other" side. Tempers were often heated and, eventually, Prattley was dubbed *persona non grata*, or PNGeed, as the jargon has it, and Operation Rainbow soon lost its gleam and momentum.

Cole Dodge of Unicef, whom we met during his work in building and running the Corridor of Peace in Uganda, was now in Khartoum and he took up the slack. He soon got things moving again through his formidable negotiating skills as a children's advocate. Dodge persuaded a suspicious government as well as a reluctant SPLA to let Unicef carry food and medicine through to children and mothers displaced and battered by the indiscriminate cruelty of the war. Dodge's aim to funnel supplies to the South as well as to the North soon ran afoul of the incipient fundamentalist movement in the North, and the Khartoum government requested Unicef to move him out. Although it was not a formal declaration that he was *persona non grata* as a representative, it amounted to that.

To be declared PNG when one is an advocate for children is taken in much of Unicef, but not in the United Nations as a whole, as a badge of honour. And so it should. Any Unicef representative who does not dare to go close to the wire, boldly but not brashly, is, in my opinion, unqualified for the job. Why did Unicef agree to move Dodge under government pressure? Jim Grant had consistently shown great forthrightness and cool clarity under the gun in similar situations when governments came down heavily on Unicef representatives. On this occasion, he agreed to move his man, presumably because the cost of making an issue of it was to risk the entire concept of the Zone of Peace for the children of the Sudan. As it turned out, the Corridors of Peace grew and Operation Rainbow was eventually transformed into Operation Lifeline Sudan (OLS), a much bigger exercise, which will be extolled in history as one of the great landmarks of humanitarian progress.

But in the interim, the whole enterprise of maintaining and running a relief corridor was being jeopardised by intransigence on both sides of the war. The SPLA launched a series of attacks on vehicles carrying supplies, alleging that they were secretly taking arms to the government forces. The government, on its part, obstreperously insisted that relief should go only to areas which it controlled, thus giving credence to the rebels' charge. The SPLA countered that if people in their areas were not to benefit, no one else would. In the 1986-7 period, several aircraft including a Unicef relief plane were shot down, barge convoys on the Nile were attacked, killing many relief workers, and the political atmosphere became increasingly explosive. The government as well as the rebels were preoccupied with killing one another and winning territory rather than with the niceties of humanitarian obligations. The numbers of civilians killed, maimed and displaced ran into the hundreds of thousands.

The sorrows of the Sudan became front-page and prime-time news: media values decree that the larger the mayhem, the bigger and more appetising the story. The Sudan government, of course, became the villain of the piece and was held responsible for the human rights violations in the country. The rebels got off relatively lightly in the media and in the world opinion the crisis had provoked. This is standard practice in the international Press which, by and large, works on the principle that in a civil war or race conflict which journalists have been parachuted in to report, the majority is always the bad guy in the black hat and the minority is the good guy in the white hat.

Pressures on the government piled up so high that in June 1988, it asked Pérez de Cuellar, the Secretary General of the United Nations, to call for a massive international relief programme to prevent starvation in the South and among the displaced people around Khartoum. De Cuellar sent a mission to the Sudan to assess the dimensions of the emergency so that he could report to the General Assembly. In October 1988, the Assembly instructed him to organise the relief and reconstruction programme in the Sudan and called for an international conference to draw urgent attention to the crisis and raise the funds needed.

This meeting, named the Conference on Relief Operations, was held in March 1989 in Khartoum under the joint aegis of the government of Sudan and the United Nations. It was co-chaired by Sudan's Minister of Social Affairs, Ahmed Abdul al-Rahman and Jim Grant. The auspices were bad. Everyone was conscious that too much time had been spent and that much suffering could have been avoided if all these frantic efforts had been made when the situation was less fraught. The SPLA, excluded from participation – they had in any case been unwilling to go with a begging bowl to Khartoum, the enemy stronghold – denounced the legality of the conference, calling it a "deep conspiracy". But following some persuasive diplomacy, they joined in the talks later. An action plan in which the UN was authorised to deal directly with the rebels was hammered together. The stage for Operation Lifeline Sudan was now set.

General Abdulrahim Farah, who played a key role in negotiating agreement of the Lifeline plan for the Sudan, commented a year later: "Lifeline showed the two sides that they were attached to the same umbilical cord. Each side claims assistance for the same people, each committed to a single Sudan. The Sudan belongs to both."

The Khartoum Accords were concluded on a relatively cordial note. The government promised to silence its guns for a whole month to let the Corridors of Peace get off to a good start and the SPLA reciprocated halfway by offering to stop shooting in agreed Corridors of Tranquillity, in gestures very reminiscent of the Days of Tranquillity in El Salvador where the whole process had begun.

Jim Grant was put in charge of Operation Lifeline Sudan as the personal representative of the Secretary General. It was a controversial appointment. Grant was widely known as a very vocal and passionate "Uniceffer", as he himself often referred to staff members and supporters of Unicef who would rather roll up their sleeves and get to work than sit behind a desk and shuffle bureaucratic bumph. Grant had a reputation for putting Unicef ahead of all other life priorities. He was a very imaginative and successful fund-raiser for children and he had proved repeatedly that he could attract the attention of the media, something that most UN agency heads longed to do but found beyond their reach. These attributes were widely admired and also widely vilified. The French – never ardent Americaphiles – called him a "cowboy"; the Swedes thought of his style of work as being akin to that of Barnum, the circus man; and other heads of UN agencies, who felt that they were being constantly upstaged by Grant, were envious of his successes and envious of the zealotry which they had never been able to produce either in themselves or in the work-ethic of their staffs.

Some members of the bigger non-governmental organisations like the Save the Children organisation in

Britain and Oxfam who had splendid records of being able to mount a delivery system in emergencies, wondered whether Grant would not hog the limelight and also the bulk of the philanthropic money that an emergency yields. And smaller private voluntary organisations, whose lifeblood is this emergency philanthropy and who had learned over the years that UN-bashing is an easy way to get themselves media notice, were quick to criticise the Secretary General for putting the head of Unicef, an institution which persistently claimed that its work for children was "above politics", in charge of an operation which was so clearly political. That kind of criticism only evokes a rather smug and tolerant ripple of risibility at Unicef which has long known that to keep children out of politics takes a great deal of political artistry. And so Jim Grant charged into action to put some "Uniceffy" life into Operation Lifeline Sudan.

Here is what Larry Minear who edited *Humanitarianism Under Siege* says about all this:

> Beyond the saga of high principle tested by day-to-day practice, Lifeline is also a story of personalities insisting that institutions live up to their missions. Lifeline reflected the passionate commitment and boundless energy of James P Grant who, as Personal Representative of the Secretary General, was perhaps its single most influential force. He made eight trips to the region in seven months to launch the initiative and keep it moving. Described in Churchillian terms by those who saw him in action, his ability to project the suffering of Sudan's civilians on to the world stage has led admirers and critics alike to resonate to the description of Lifeline as "humanitarian theatre".

This is felicitously said. But to leave it like that is to unwittingly belittle the drama of Operation Lifeline Sudan and to underplay the character and substantive work of the protagonist depicted in those few lines cited above. There were many dimensions to the script – many of which have been ably and judiciously described in *Humanitarianism Under Siege*. One of the most important for the record, and for the future possibilities of giving additional experiential substance to Nils Thedin's humanitarian wish that children would be treated by the world as a Zone of Peace protected from the wars that adults fight around them, is the recognition by both the government and the rebels in the Sudan that while engaged in a brutal fight for their political "rights", they had humane obligations towards the next generation of Sudanese: children and the mothers who nurtured them through their dependent years.

Another noteworthy dimension of the drama was the emergence of a new diplomacy, personified by Jim Grant and his colleagues such as Winston Prattley who succeeded Grant as Personal Representative of the Secretary General; Cole Dodge; Vincent O'Reilly; Mary Racellis; Farid Rahman; Thomas Ekvall of Unicef; many other frontline workers in the High Commission for Refugees, the World Food Programme and the UN Development Programme; and indomitable men and women in non-governmental organisations who undertook many dangerous assignments with no other motive except humanitarian service. The new diplomacy which Jim Grant practised was more direct, more immediate and more head-to-head than the traditional mincing which has been the accepted style of statecraft from Kautilya to Kissinger. The most effective instance is the extraordinary success of making it possible for Lifeline to ride the turbulent wave of political change caused by the top-pling of the government of Prime Minister Sadiq al-Mahdi, who had presided over its beginning in a military-led *coup d'état* led by Lieutenant-General Omar Hassan Ahmed al-Bashir, barely three months after the Khar-toum Accords were entered into, legitimising the Zones of Tranquillity. On the very day that al-Bashir took power, Jim Grant was in his office urging him to maintain the humanitarian principle of Zones of Peace for children.

Al-Bashir agreed immediately and even approved of Grant going on to meet John Garang, the rebel leader in the South, to reaffirm his commitment to the principle of Zones of Peace for children and the operations of Oper-ation Lifeline Sudan. This was probably the first time in the history of international diplomacy that a United Nations official treated directly with a rebel leader. It was achieved with the compliance of the head of state so that there was no violation of the sanctity of the UN prin-ciple of sovereignty. This departure from established practice says something for the character not only of Jim Grant but also of al-Bashir and the ethos of the Sudanese people who have managed to preserve their fine sense of human graciousness under the pressure of interminable brutish warfare and relentless poverty.

To many who have applauded the spirit and perform-ance of Lifeline, it seemed that apart from the primary business of delivering food, medicines and vaccines, the very fact that it was able to secure the willing cooper-ation (albeit occasionally flawed) of both sides who were not at all comfortable with the mounting sufferings of the civilian population, particularly the children of the Sudan, proved that out of the blood and gore of the war it is possible for human beings to bring out their essential humaneness not just for display but for positive action.

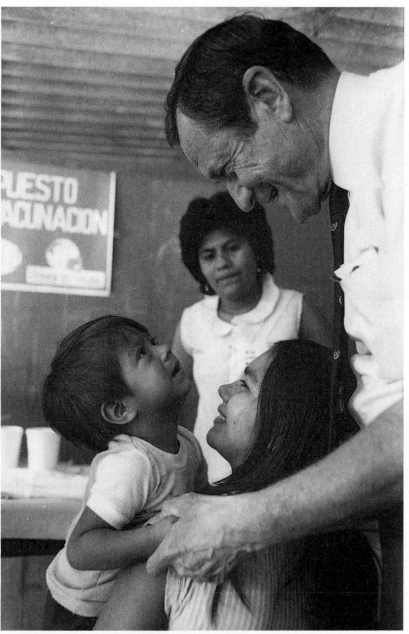

Unicef's Executive Director, James Grant, at a temporary vaccination post in El Salvador, where 400,000 children were inoculated.

UNICEF/1091/Dennis Budd Gray

Teenagers participating in the Education for Peace Volunteer
Development camp in Daroun, north-east of Beirut.

UNICEF/5215/Nicole Toutonji

Children prepare games for the Farewell Bazaar that closes their
programme at Abaye Education for Peace Camp, Beirut.

UNICEF/5231/Nicole Toutonji

The photograph which turned the world's hearts against war: South Vietnamese forces follow terrified children after an accidental aerial Napalm strike.   *Photo by Huynh Cong "Nick" UT*

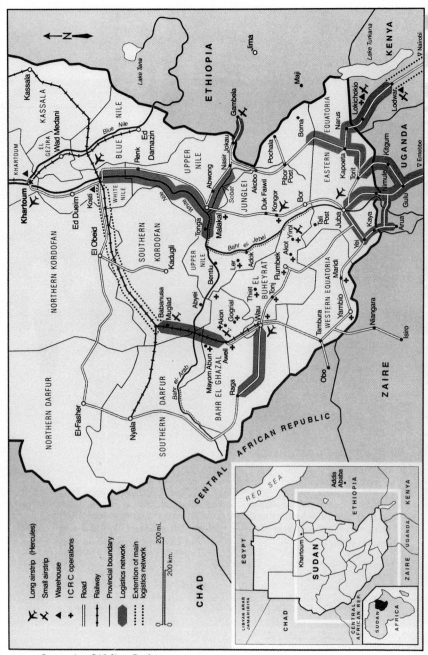

Operation Lifeline Sudan

Operation Lifeline Sudan: a long awaited food train, delivering food and emergency supplies arrives in Aweil. *UNICEF/Jeremy Hartley*

A girl cares for her sibling at a Unicef assisted feeding centre for drought-affected people, in the southern city of Juba.
UNICEF/ Roger Lemoyne

The sea corridor of peace: children and women evacuated from Dubrovnik on the hydrofoil, arrive in Bari, Italy.   *UNICEF/Laurent Delhalle*

James Grant visiting war-traumatised children in a refugee centre in the town of Sremska Mitrovica, Serbia.   *UNICEF/5431/John Isaac*

Abdul Mohammed
*With the kind
permission of
Abdul Mohammed*

Monsenor Arturo
Rivera Damas
UNICEF

Nils Thedin

Photo by Ruby Mera

UNICEF
Executive
Director
James Grant
*UNICEF/DIR 91-2-3/
Joe Rubino*

But to the fundamentalists of the North who watched these actions with some sharp-edged scepticism, Lifeline, and the humanitarian impulse behind it, seemed to be value-loaded against the development of Islam.

Now let us count some of the human and political gains from Operation Lifeline Sudan and meet some of the concerns of its critics. Perhaps the most important of the many gains was the reaffirmation this experience offered that humane ideas about peace and responsibility stemming from enduring values such as caring for children in trouble, especially children without parents, still prevail in the human consciousness in spite of the evidence everywhere that the beast in man continues to co-exist with the angel within. People who had been increasingly secularised over the past 300 years and who had abandoned their churches and temples in droves – as well as the values their foreparents had cleft to for two or three thousand years, albeit erratically – responded generously when they were informed that hundreds of thousands of African children were moving about the arid landscape in search of food and water and that famine was stalking them close on their heels. Some $300m. were quickly contributed when the United Nations put out the first appeal for the Sudan. There are two pre-conditions, it seems, to evoke such swift and generous responses: credible information through the public media, and credible relief institutions which have a reputation for being honest and capable of using the money well. Time and time again, people have proved that the wells of human caring within them are profound. Such notions as "aid fatigue" seem to be glib inventions of journalists who are trapped in a system of values which require them to drop a subject after a day or a few weeks at the most, and move on to some other breathless event. They coined the phrase more to vindicate their own short attention-span than as a reflection of the flightiness of the public conscience.

Reporting the processes which give rise to events such as famine, and doing it as grippingly and skillfully as the Press cooks its daily menu of ephemera, is not in the training manuals nor the professional ethos of the media. Obsolescence is built into their product. Unfortunately such slick tag-lines as "aid-fatigue" infect the minds of the bureaucrats of the donor agencies who are constantly on the look-out for new projects and programmes in which to invest, ventures which promise new yields which they can claim are more immediately fruitful and different from the pet schemes of their predecessors in office. The periodicity of organised philanthropy is a subject which I highly recommend for a PhD thesis. The psychological need for every head of a social-welfare ministry and agency to do something "different" during his or her tenure of office seems to be an ineluctable natural law. It is an expensive pastime and an immoral one, considering that the stakes are human lives and public money.

Yet, in a complex operation like OLS, how do you measure success? In a knotted web of social disorder in which the civilian population, especially women and children, are being brutalised, what are the criteria of "success"? If the food and medical supplies needed to prevent the looming famine and pestilence confronting millions of Sudanese people were delivered as planned – and, remarkably, in the case of Operation Lifeline Sudan they were – is it not mere cavilling or just a lofty intellectual exercise to ask, as indeed some do, whether OLS could have been designed differently so as to increase the capacity of Sudan to deal adequately with future emergencies or some such weighty consideration? But, in the event, apart from averting a second Holocaust soon after the disaster which struck the Horn of Africa and the Sahel in 1984-5, there were other important human gains from OLS, largely in the lessons to be learnt from the actors playing their roles in that vast human drama.

Perhaps one of the most important lessons, the nature of which is not yet understood though it keeps being repeated over and over again, is that there is an ugly phenomenon which may be called competitive philanthropy that arises frequently when humanitarian intervention by the international community takes place. There are two broad categories of institutions involved in this mêlée: the intergovernmental agencies of the United Nations system; and the non-governmental organisations ranging from globe-wide bodies such as the International Red Cross, Oxfam, the ring of national Save the Children Funds and Médecins Sans Frontières to the smaller and more recently established private voluntary organisations of enthusiastic activists preoccupied with particular aspects of emergencies. A generalised *modus vivendi* has existed for four decades within these two categories and between them. But this loose live-and-let-live arrangement has only worked fitfully. Without denigrating the tremendous value of the services of many of these voluntary agencies, it must be said that some of them, particularly the smaller ones whose bread and butter are funds generated by emergencies, quickly learned the cute trick of getting media attention by taking swipes at the UN agencies, easy targets for criticism, especially during the Nixon and Reagan regimes when pseudo-intellectual Ku-Klux-Klans like the Heritage Foundation began burning metaphorical crosses on the UN's lawns. Almost always, the burden of the criticism is that the UN has been late in getting in on the action. It was thus in Uganda, in Kampuchea, in Mozambique, in Iraq, and in the Sudan.

It is a credible criticism and a valid one because the international agencies, by the very nature of their mandates and by their size, move cumbrously and portentously. They are bound by the sovereignty principle, which is entrenched in the UN charter, to respect national borders and the autonomy of member states. Only recently in international relations has the notion become increasingly predominant that sovereign nations have not only rights but obligations towards people within their borders, and that their governments cannot abuse with impunity the ethos of universal human rights, which most of them have agreed to in a variety of Declarations and Conventions. Apartheid provided the first progressive breach in the absolute interpretation of national sovereignty.

It was unfortunate that for many decades during which the case for principled intervention was taking root, the United States in particular, and the other permanent members in general, resorted to the United Nations' good offices only when it suited the political purposes of their governments – as in the cases of the Falklands, Angola, Afghanistan and Nicaragua – taking direct action rather than seeking agreement from other members. One reason was self-interest, and the other was their conviction that the United Nations was far too embattled in ideological schisms to be able to reach common agreement on any major issue. The most recent examples of the advancement of the interventionist principle were offered by Iraq's invasion of Kuwait, and Saddam Hussein's cruelty towards the Kurds and the Shiites; Yugoslavia's internecine barbarity; and the clan warfare within Somalia which brought its four million people to the abyss of famine.

A succession of such interventionist experiences may be the price humanity has to pay to learn that the sovereign-state idea cannot prevail permanently over the principle of "One World, One Human Race". It is essential to restore the human values which have been discarded in the interest of sovereign governments bolstered by the new religion of "pragmatism" – an ethic that originally meant "state interest". That may well be the only way for United Nations agencies concerned with emergencies and disaster-relief to have their mandates revised and strengthened to enable them to act to prevent suffering when possible and to move swiftly to intervene when suffering is already blighting people's lives.

5
Through the Corridor

They told me that some 9,000 Sudanese boys, from eight to thirteen years of age, had gathered near a township called Narus, some twenty kilometres from Kenya's northern border. Unaccompanied by their parents, they had walked there from Ethiopia – the last leg of a 1,400-mile journey which they had begun some six to eight years before, from Khartoum and other places in North Sudan, to escape from the ravages of the civil war, to get away from the boredom of their daily cattle-herding chores, or simply to join their friends, as they variously explained. Unicef staff members and non-governmental organisations who had helped them along their trek offered another reason: they were being recruited as candidate guerrillas by the Sudan People's Liberation Army.

This was the view of the government of Sudan whose Minister for Social Welfare and Development, Dr Hussein Abu Saleh, explained that the boys were being detained by the rebels not only to train and brainwash them to serve as gofers and actual fighters for their cause but also to act as magnets for the relief supplies which they expected the boys to attract. The SPLA, of course, gave a very different explanation. Government attacks on their villages had separated them from their families and sent them trekking in search of food and security.

The government's story, ironically, is reinforced by spokesmen of a break-away faction of the SPLA who asserted that agents of the main group led by John Garang had intimidated village leaders to separate thousands of young boys from their parents, gather them in platoons, and pack them off to refugee camps in Mengistu's Ethiopia where they received some formal schooling as well as guerrilla training and indoctrination. The older boys were trained with real guns, the younger boys with sticks. The truth, as in all confused human situations, may be a mixture of all these contradictory stories.

The refugee camps at Itang, Panyido and Dima in Ethiopia were set up and administered by the Communist government of President Mengistu which was politically aligned with the SPLA and hostile to the Khartoum regime. When Mengistu fell to the onslaught of the Ethiopian People's Revolutionary Democratic Front in May 1991, the refugee camps were broken up and the inmates fled across the nearest Sudanese border some 100 kilometres away. They first sought refuge at Pakok and then at Gorkuo. But these havens, poor as they were, came constantly under attack and they had to flee again. During that hurried trek they were set upon by Toposa tribesmen. Five children were killed and several others wounded. They marched to the southern town of Kapoeta in batches of 2,000 protected by armed SPLA fighters. Eventually, they were trucked to Narus, where I was headed that day.

They had been at Narus for several weeks, without a scrap of shelter or adequate food, water or clothing. I had to see them for myself and to ask them how they had endured their long trek and how they were subsisting. More than anything else I needed to talk to them about how they felt about being so long on the run without their mothers and fathers, what they felt they needed most, what their persistent dreams were.

I asked Thomas Ekvall at the regional Unicef office in Nairobi, a young Swede who was responsible for Operation Lifeline Sudan's southern sector operations, to brief me about these unaccompanied minors. He offered to take me to Narus. During the flight in a small Unicef plane from Nairobi to Lokichokio, the northernmost township on the border, Ekvall made it plain that he was no romantic believer in the good intentions of either the government or the rebels. He was convinced, he told me, that both sides would seize whatever could be turned to advantage, including those youngsters. He warned me repeatedly that the boys had been brainwashed by the SPLA and would parrot what they had been taught to say by the Sudan People's Liberation Army. Ekvall was a water expert who had originally been hired to drill wells and provide clean drinking water for children in the Sudan. This was his first experience as a manager of a "Corridor of Peace" for children. Through his experience as a water engineer in Juba and southern Sudan, he had come to know the land and its peculiarities, its bounty and its harshness, and he was deeply saddened by the depleting effects on it from two decades of warfare between the Muslim North and the largely Christian South. He knew personally John Garang and other rebel leaders of the Sudan People's Liberation Army and its civilian wing, the Sudan People's Liberation Movement which was widely suspected of being touched by the sort of Stalinist Communism espoused by Haile Mariam Mengistu, the deposed President of Ethiopia.

Ekvall was a natural-born sceptic, preferring to judge people by their actions rather than their words, and he understood the nuances of the political idiom which both sides in the civil war used. He would have been a first-rate journalist, but he was deeply distrustful of the Press. He avoided contact with journalists and was reluctant even to hold a Press Conference – one of the necessary duties of the manager of a Zone of Peace for children, as Cole Dodge had shown by his valuable relationship with journalists, particularly foreign correspondents reporting the Ugandan civil war. But Ekvall was afraid that his statements would be distorted – as they frequently had been – and as a junior bureaucrat, he found himself answerable for his statements to many bosses not only in Unicef in Nairobi and Khartoum but also in New York. Donor governments too had people moving around in Africa and they were constantly demanding "accountability" and trying to micro-manage the programmes they supported. There is probably no more unattractive and crass a figure than the piper insistently calling for his tune to be played, even if that tune is harsh in the ears of his audience.

Realising that Thomas Ekvall was a very private person with special expertise which, on the face of it, seemed not to qualify him for crisis management, as that calls for political adroitness and quick improvisation, I wondered whether he was miscast in his current role. I was soon reassured. On the ground, at the camp shared by Unicef and the World Food Programme in Lokichokio, there was an urgent radio message for Ekvall. The way he responded to it gave me the real measure of his value as an emergency manager and as a human being. The emergency call had come from colleagues working deep in southern Sudan, near the town of Kapoeta. The rains had ceased and the government army, which could not easily operate with their heavy equipment on those mud roads, was thrusting forward from north to south. Seven UN colleagues and two workers for a non-governmental relief organisation were caught in the middle. They wanted to be taken out of their predicament to be able to rest, regroup and return when the time was more propitious.

There was a twin-engine plane at hand and three pilots: an American woman and two young Ethiopians. With great aplomb, Ekvall gave them a test and some practice in what they needed to do as though he had been a "Search-and-Rescue" man all his life. He told them that he had given radio instructions to his marooned colleagues to select a stretch of reasonable flat dirt roadway, lop off any intrusive tree branches, and clearly mark the ends of an improvised airstrip. The pilots rehearsed the approach, flying for many miles at no more than ten to fifteen feet above the ground to avoid being sighted by army troops and also to duplicate the actual conditions in which the rescue would take place. Ekvall also had a gender-politics decision to make. Under Unicef's current ethos, women had to be given preference if their qualifications were the same as a male competitor for any job. He tried out all three and selected the two Ethiopians. Not because of their gender but because their low-flying performances were better. They also had experience of flying over similar terrain. Then he radioed his colleagues over the border and told them that the plane would be coming in about three o'clock that afternoon.

Without any awkwardness about failing in his caretaker responsibilities towards me, he told me that he had decided to fly with the pilots. I asked him why. He said that the people they were rescuing would feel better if they saw that he was willing to share the risks they had been asked to take. I told him that I would make the cross-border journey without him and he arranged for another water engineer – a marvellously weather-beaten Californian – to accompany me in a Unicef Land-Rover, across the Kenya-Sudan border and into Narus and back.

The thoughts predominant in my mind just then were not about Zones of Peace, the tribulations of those parentless children or of the rescue itself, but about the special quality of the men and women who worked for Unicef, especially in emergencies. Just as Unesco has done superbly what it is best at – resurrecting and maintaining ancient monuments, Unicef has always done its best work in children's emergencies ever since its establishment in 1946 as the United Nations International Children's Emergency Fund. (It has called itself the United Nations Children's Fund since 1952 when it was reconceived as a development agency for children.)

I saw the rescue plane flying north as I began my trip without any visas or any of those nasty documents which modern travellers are compelled to show to at least five border officials wherever they moved in this so-called "global village". There was a lone Kenyan customs officer whose permission I needed to proceed. He came up to the Land-Rover and said: "Go with your soul and return with your soul." And he waved me on. His blessing touched me where I needed it. There is a sort of wisdom, a kind of unadorned spiritual grandeur, in simple people who have not been corrupted by the sophistication which is so highly prized in smart society, people who have not become victims of the egoistic need to project an image of status or power which comes from the authority of a uniform or an official rank or the barrel of a gun. This man knew that I was on my way to Narus on what some, rather pompously, would term a "humanitarian mission" and he had sensed my anxieties about venturing into the harsh unknown.

The road was deeply rutted and potholed. Uninhabited scrubland stretched as far as I could see. The water engineer and I talked about Africa and the terrible things people were doing to each other and their children. He too had worked in the Horn and knew that much of the horrors the survivors had endured for decades were the fallout of Cold War geopolitics. Remote-control power games played in Washington and Moscow had destroyed any early possibility that Ethiopia, Somalia, the Sudan and Angola in the west could develop their own democratic systems of governance and build a future for their children. The destruction of the environment in the Horn and in the Sahel was largely due to the governments of those areas being lured by arms and by bribes to play alien war-games, while the children, except those of the élite groups who were participants, were losing their ecological heritage, their chances for an education and all prospects of a decent future. Similarly, Mozambique had been driven into an ugly civil war by the remote-control actions of South Africa. And, as an eye-opening tract issued by Unicef termed it, "children on the frontline" were the principal victims. They were losing not only what they had, but also what they were entitled by their humanity to have: a future. It seemed to us, rocking along in that vehicle, that war, war of any kind – international, civil, or holy, or for whatever "cause" – was unjustifiable because with modern weapons and strategies, more than eighty per cent of its victims are not soldiers but civilians, and more than half of them are children. It seemed to us that there is no such thing as a "Just War", however blaring the propaganda. There is no human reason to kill a child. People have children. Governments don't. People don't go to war. Governments do.

These ruminations brought us to Narus. Imagine seeing a long wall of young black heads and bodies, mobilised to greet the Land-Rover. They did not know we were coming. But any visitor was welcome. Imagine also that there was no din, though the children were talking to one another. There were 9,000 of them. A group of twenty kids from New York would create an ear-splitting pandemonium if they were brought together in one space without supervision, I thought. And imagine that there was not a single child with palms outstretched to beg for food. All stereotypes in my mind were belied at once. These children who had been through many tribulations and through hell itself had learned to respect themselves and also one another. They were disciplined by life-experience, but not by imposition from above. I had brought no gifts, no food, no tents; just a pad of paper. I walked through the multitude and asked the French voluntary workers who had taken up the cause of these children why there were no girls in the group. They told me that Sudanese girls stay with their mothers whatever happens. They are the prospective brides who would attract a dowry, perhaps of several heads of cattle or a piece of land; they were the fetchers of firewood and water, the energy source of the poor; and they were the future bearers of the children needed to perpetuate the family and its clan. As I am Sri Lankan, most of this was familiar to me. The absence of girls from the refugee camps was no great mystery and did not add up to "proof", as a Sudanese government official suggested, that the boys had been corralled for recruitment by the rebels.

As I walked around, I observed that many of the children were busy cooking their handful of maize or chickpeas in small fish-cans held over tiny fires made out of dried leaves and twigs. This was going to be their dinner. And, suddenly, hundreds of faces were looking up skyward. A dense black cloud had appeared just above their camp, targeting them for a downpour minutes later. The boys had no tents or other shelter. They went about collecting dried branches from the scrubland, tenting them with large leaves sewn together with small pieces of twig. There was no excitement, just an increased pace of activity in order to cope with another problem in their young lives. I picked a thirteen-year-old youngster who did not seem to be too busy and took him into the hut in which the voluntary workers had made their office, kitchen and home.

His name was John Awak. Did he know who his parents were? Joseph and Adhar Kondok. Where was their home? In Gogrial, near Khartoum. What was he doing before he left home? Minding the cattle. Did he not want to return home to his parents? Why had he left home? Because his father had gone to the war and his mother was not able to look after him. And also he wanted to escape the war and the drought with a group of friends. Yes, he would like to see his parents again – he had not seen them for nearly four years – but he did not want to return to the same life again as a cattle-herder. What did he dream about mostly? What dreams came more than once? A schoolroom, he replied. Why a schoolroom? Because when he and his friends went to Ethiopia during the Mengistu regime, there were some nice "white people" who had arranged for a school for them where they learned to become "something different". This was the camp at Dima, in western Ethiopia. They had been given food and medicine when they became sick. Enquiries made later showed that these "nice white people" were from Rada Barnen, the Swedish Save the Children organisation which Nils Thedin, the inspiration for these Zones of Peace, had headed for many years. I asked John Awak whether there was something I could give him now or have it sent on to him later. He pointed to my yellow pad and my ball-point pen. I handed them over. Then he thanked me and ran off, as children will, to get to work at once with his new possessions.

I asked several other children about their dreams and longings. Most of them dreamed of a school where they would learn to read and to write. When I talked to the voluntary workers, they whispered that this was an example of brainwashing by the SPLA personnel who had escorted the boys from Ethiopia to Narus. This, I was told, was a part of their disciplinary training for recruitment in the rebel army. These explanations reinforced Thomas Ekvall's warnings about taking the word of these boys too seriously. But a reporter, with all his scepticism, learns to look for subtler indications in what people are than in what they say: the look on the face, the movement of the eyes, the tone of the voice, the rapidity of the response to a question. And also to look for the simpler rather than the more complicated explanation when they talk to children because, as Roger Rosenblatt reported in his little masterpiece, *Children of War*, children prefer not to tell lies. Lies are too complicated. The truth is always simple. Why could not both suppositions be true? Why could it not be SPLA training ("other people brainwash, we train") as well as a genuine wish for education, to become "something different", in the minds of these boys?

My explanation to myself was that the only happy days they remembered was in the Rada Barnen school which had given them a framework for their days, food for their hunger, a bed for their tiredness, and a hope for a "different" life through education. Could that not be the explanation of those recurrent dreams? The reluctance to accept the simple assertion that a school was the dearest wish of these boys may also be attributed to the fear that if a school were built at the camp, it would make it more likely that the camp site would become permanent. That would mean that the refugee children would become permanent dependants on the agencies who are now supporting them, who prefer to work on the supposition that things will change for the better sooner rather than later and that they could go on to do other things, other good deeds elsewhere. Good deeds need money and money has to be raised. Besides, even good deeds, repeated over and over, become boring.

The black cloud broke and spilt its contents over Narus. The children got a soaking but they chose to enjoy the bathing rather than complain. We left the camp soon after, knowing that the roads would be much worse than they had been on the outward journey. They were. The long ruts made by wheel tracks had turned into russet rills of slushy mud. In the huge ruts in the road the water was a foot deep. It took all the strength of the driver to keep us from sliding into the fields below. I understood why an army equipped with heavy trucks and armour tries to avoid the rainy season. Bad weather is always on the side of the more agile guerrillas who have very light equipment to carry and can use light vehicles like ordinary cars, jeeps, ox-carts or even Shanks's pony for their treks into enemy territory.

It took us three hours to return to Lokichokio and to greet Ekvall and the relief workers he had brought out of Sudan. The exercise had gone exactly according to his plan. The Ethiopian pilots had flown at ten feet for long stretches as though they were piloting a ground-skimming Ibis rather than a two-engine aircraft. That evening we drank some beer to celebrate, played some chess and talked about Operation Lifeline Sudan. It had already become a part of the lives of the men and women working on the project. It was very different from life at Unicef headquarters in New York or at its European office in Geneva, where bureaucracy, paper-pushing and meetings are the order of the day. Those people out there work day and night and have the satisfaction as Thomas Ekvall did that evening, of seeing today's work pay dividends for children today rather than at the invisible end of some planned rainbow or "Development Decade". The work of a Unicef emergency field worker is certainly unorthodox, sometimes dangerous and always a bit catch-as-catch-can, as it would seem to one of those inspectors sent by donor governments to do what they call their "monitoring and evaluating". But there is a ready return for the client: the children at the end of a Corridor of Peace. And there is a sort of grim fun in putting oneself in discomfort and at risk while improvising, learning and practising the art of winning the trust of strangers in the villages, of the bureaucrats who infest every country, and of the men at the top planning and plotting to kill one another in a civil war. The frequent fear, the occasional terror, the boredom of waiting, the pain of holding down one's irritability when incompetence and dishonesty get in the way, cannot be monitored or evaluated. It has to be experienced and felt.

6
War In The Minds of Children

Perhaps the single most important cause of our obsession with war throughout history is that we forget how we felt about the external world when we were children. Very occasionally, as adult men and women, we receive illuminating flashes of memory from that obscure past. They take the form of pictures and the feelings which accompanied them. The earliest pictures of childhood are black and white, light and shade with no fear staining the faces and places of the experience. There are some sounds too: a woman singing, someone playing piano scales next door, a motor engine revving up, perhaps bird sounds in the eaves, the rustling of leaves. Then, at around age six or seven, about the time of the tooth fairy and school entrance, the pictures change. The lightness is gone. The faces and places are tinged with sadness, and the feeling is corrupted with fear. They are like pictures of rumours, unpleasant and hurtful to someone. Remembered sounds of parents quarrelling, whispers of the death of a grandparent, of the death of a child in the neighbourhood. There is also a smell coating the images. Often it is the smell of fear. It is remembered as an infection, a reflection within of the fear in the eyes of the grown-ups in the house.

In those very early years, time was always today. There was no past and no future. You woke up and the time was now. And now was there till you went to bed. Time was vertical, not horizontal as it is in history which is concerned with serial time. Adult time is a river of human experience carrying the story of mankind's passions: love turning to indifference, tenderness turning sour, aspirations becoming blunted, greed for power escalating into war, understanding destroyed by miscommunication – the terrible habit of using the same words to mean different things. There were also times to look forward to, moments of intense wonderment, time here and now and, therefore, times of revelation and inspiration. St Augustine's time. God's time. Vertical, instantaneous time, but flowing, like early childhood's time. But those moments become rarer as the river nears the ocean.

At twelve and thirteen begins the period of adolescent and adult memory-pictures which are almost always soiled with attachments to something wanted from the future, to acquire knowledge for a future purpose and not for itself and for now, to search for external stimuli, not to be more alive as one is, but to be "taken out of" oneself and identified with the person on the screen or the words of that song or the "elsewhere" in which one would rather be than here where one is. That is the first experience of boredom.

Now, in adulthood, the early memories have been suppressed deep in the mind, but not erased. They are there, but not reachable at will. It is almost impossible to touch and relive those picture-memories of very young life in which there was no fear because there was no cause for fear. You recall only the later pictures in which rumours and reports of war and of violence were commonplace. They have become a part of your recallable past and therefore of your reality. The pictures and their sounds suggest that war and its violence are epic deeds of humankind, that war brings out the best in us – comradeship, inventiveness, courage and a myriad other heroic virtues which are appropriate for emulation.

But those time-categories of childhood memories are becoming less valid now. War and violence are no longer sounds of distant thunder. They are everywhere, around the homes of children and in their homes where television insists that violence is the only interesting way of life and that the critics of gory entertainment are blue-nosed prudes. We train children in every aspect of life except how to read a newspaper or watch television discriminatingly so that they do not identify completely with the figures on the screen, absorbing the unhuman values of violence and war which are being projected at them every second. We do not do this because we ourselves do not know how to avoid being victimised by the demons of the box.

The answer to this malefic influence is not censorship but education in the art of reading and watching television with critical eyes. But we do not dare to propose this because we ourselves are addicted and we have a strong tendency to imagine that little children are mindless creatures whose daily experience is erased by sleep. So a little tele-violence may not be too harmful. That proposition may have been true fifty years ago but it is no longer true when the imagery of reality is so powerful and impressive. It is absorbed by the senses and embossed on the mind. Hundreds of clinical studies on mental trauma of children caught in the crossfire of adult violence have established that these experiences have long-term effects on children, perhaps even permanent effects, unless they are therapeutically understood and treated early.

At the University of Edinburgh, work is being done on measuring the bio-chemical impact on children's minds of the trauma of war. There is some evidence that suggests there are measurable changes in the brain chemistry caused by traumatic fears, even about the war that has not yet taken place: Armageddon. Clinical studies of childhood trauma – largely the work of academics and non-governmental groups – have been undertaken in the Lebanon, the Philippines, Sri Lanka, Nicaragua, Israel and in the occupied territories of Palestine, where children have been on the frontlines of state terrorism as well as "civilian" terrorism. The trauma is expressed through broken sleep and nightmares; irritability and excessive quarrelsomeness with friends; protracted preoccupied moods which amount to "switching off" from current surroundings and context; crayon drawings of bombers, guns and other deadly weapons; and, occasionally, in speech.

Reaching Children in War lists these traumatic responses of children exposed to violence: fear and anxiety; intrusive images and thoughts; difficulties in concentrating, particularly at school; a sense of isolation; chronic sadness and depression; avoidance behaviour; a sense of guilt that they were not able to help in preventing the death of a brother, sister, parent or friend (perhaps they would agree to add guilt for having survived); re-enactment of the traumatic event in play and artistic expression; sleep disturbances and nightmares and, of course, the physical damage they themselves suffered.

They comment: "Although these memories become less frequent over time, for many children they remain unless they have had the opportunity to talk or play them

93

through." Alas, most of them will not have this opportunity because during continuing conflicts, those who
might be able to help them to expunge the wounds in
their minds are usually preoccupied with emergency
feeding and physical medication, as in the case of the Pal-
estinian children whose limbs had been deliberately
broken to stop them from throwing stones during the In-
tifada. Dodge and Raundalen offer one glimmer of hope:
they suggest that although traumatised children do not
easily forget, there is little or no evidence of a desire for
vengeance in the minds of the children they studied in
Ulster, the Lebanon, the Sudan, Mozambique or Uganda.
Evidently children have to be taught and re-taught to
hate.

The most compelling account that I have read about
children traumatised by war in a growing library of
studies is Roger Rosenblatt's *Children of War* in which he
spoke with children who had been knocked about by the
brutality of years of living with shells and bullets flying
around them in Ireland, the Lebanon, Palestine, Israel,
Kampuchea and Vietnam. This small book (published by
Doubleday) needs to be read by every adult as a gem of
empathetic reporting, the work of a fine journalist who is
not frightened of being considered a bleeding heart by his
colleagues who generally hide their humanity under a
carapace of facile cynicism. Rosenblatt's observations on
children as a superbly reliable source of truth are revela-
tions.

> Children make terrible liars on the whole, not
> because they have a more heightened sense of
> morality than adults but because they pay such
> absolute attention to the truth that a lie becomes an
> insult to their sense of appreciation. It is as though

they lie poorly as an apology to the truth. When they are not lying and are thus uncomfortable, they usually let themselves go totally. You see, this happened, then that happened, and it was all astonishing.

Children like to deal in abstractions, says Rosenblatt. They may draw them from the lines and dots they take in, but the process is mysterious and labyrinthine. The product, however, is stunningly clear, which is why children make better witnesses to the truth than to the facts.

This distinction, in my opinion, is vital to understand the nature of the media and the channels through which we receive the "knowledge" we use to appreciate what is going on around us. Facts and truths are but remote cousins. As adults we know this well. In our self-proclaimed search for the "truth" that is already present in our mind-sets, we select the facts which vindicate our truth. Very young children are still free of mind-sets – tuned to our prejudices. Racism, for instance, or skin-colour preferences, are not native: they are inserted by adults, not necessarily deliberately but by conversations overheard or by the behavioural instructions people give to children: don't play with the kids down the street, they are different, they carry germs, et cetera. Those kids down the street are also black or brown or yellow in skin colour and are designated as "Afro-Americans" or Mexicans, Puerto Ricans or Asians. Children make the links easily between the "bad" business of spreading germs and the people responsible who are identifiable by their pigmentation – dark, white or yellow – or cast of eye – "slinky" or "slit" – or whatever. The popular notion that racism and xenophobia are inborn – a conclusion drawn from the "fact" that such attitudes are widely prevalent and therefore deemed to be universal – does not stand up when one looks clearly at the behaviour of the innocents.

Rodgers and Hammerstein understood well that these attitudes, which later become the causes of "ethnic" and "cultural-linguistic" conflicts when children grow into adults, are taught as "facts" to young minds which innately "know" the truth that there is only one human race:

> You've got to be taught to hate and fear,
> You've got to be taught from year to year,
> It's got to be drummed in your dear little ear –
> You've got to be carefully taught.
>
> You've got to be taught to be afraid
> Of people whose eyes are oddly made
> And people whose skin is a different shade –
> You've got to be carefully taught.
>
> You've got to be taught
> Before it's too late,
> Before you are six
> Or seven or eight,
> To hate all the people your relatives hate –
> You've got to be carefully taught,
> You've got to be carefully taught.
>
> (*South Pacific*)

The insertion of lies into the minds of small children is the first trauma they experience: the clash between what they innately sense as that abstraction called the truth and the lie they are taught as the fact. From then on a succession of lies are taught which traumatise young minds incessantly in the efforts of adults to teach *their* reality to their children by the facile device of dividing people into We and They, Us and Them, Ours and Theirs, Our Religion and Their Religion, Our God and Their God, Our People and Their People, and of course, Our Country and Their Country. So Woody Guthrie sang gloriously of his magical "fact": "This land is my land, this land is your land ... This land was made for you and me." The implication now being drawn is: not for "Them", not for the stranger. The welcoming embrace of the giant green lady in New York harbour is not so welcoming now to the "huddled masses" whose eyes are oddly made or whose skins are a different shade.

Harold Wilson, the British Prime Minister was loth to send the military to Southern Rhodesia (now Zimbabwe) to quell the rebellion of Ian Smith who had proclaimed his Unilateral Declaration of Independence from Britain because, as Wilson explained, the white settlers were "kith and kin". That is, Our People who were white, in contrast to Their People who were black. The British government had no qualms at all in sending forces to Kenya to quell the Mau Mau rebellion led by Jomo Kenyatta.

It would be another lie to leave the impression that these prejudices inserted in the minds of children always, or generally, are crimes committed against humanity by only Americans and Europeans. Prejudice, often vicious, not just against the "whites" but against other people with dark skin shades and casts of eye, is rampant in Asia and Africa. It is a rare Indian (or Sri Lankan) family who would comfortably take in a black African as a member of their extended family. And when it comes to marriage, the prejudicial discrimination becomes much narrower so that the choice of partners is still usually confined by ethnic, religious, caste and, of course, class considerations to avoid the tainting of "pure" breeding.

Tribalism, clannism, casteism, ethnicism, linguism and religionism as devices to attain political and economic power for one or other group of élites is at present being taught by word and by ambient experience as one of the bases of popular education in scores of countries in the southern hemisphere as well as in the northern.

To find just one example of rampant political tribalism, we have only to look at the ugly relationship between India and neighbouring Sri Lanka during the Rajiv Gandhi premiership. When he felt his grasp on the reins of India slipping, Gandhi had no compunction about sending the Indian Air Force across the Palk Straits to drop "humanitarian bombs" of food and medicine over the Jaffna Peninsula where the militant Tamil Tigers were fighting the predominantly Sinhalese army of the Sri Lanka government. The Tamils of Sri Lanka had suddenly become Gandhi's "kith and kin" because there were sixty million Tamils in South India who needed to be politically appeased by a display of ethnic solidarity.

This tribal view of the world is at the base of most of the violence which maims, kills and traumatises small children. There is no "final" way, it seems, to protect children from the violence of adults except by an effective "One World" ethos and by the institutions necessary to banish war as a permissible way to resolve human disputes in our time when war weapons, nuclear as well as non-nuclear, have become catastrophically lethal not only to armies but to civilians.

When the United Nations was built on First Avenue in New York, a group of Jews and Christians who felt alike etched those beautiful words from the vision of the Prophet Isaiah on the curved wall near the steps going up into 43rd Street across UN Plaza:

They shall beat their swords into ploughshares, and

their spears into pruning hooks: nation shall not lift up sword against nation, neither shall they learn war any more.

Any thought that such an idea – the abolition of war – is practicable and acceptable in the modern world will undoubtedly and promptly be rejected by many people who read this book as a utopian hope which cannot be taken seriously by anyone except the most ingenious. Yet such utopian ideas, widely regarded as impossibly naive, have changed history. They are the flavour and very substance of the Charter of the United Nations. Did the founders of the United Nations believe their own words? Did "we the people", in whose name they signed the charter and cheered the act as a magnificent sign that they and their children would be spared the "scourge of war", believe that those ideas were impracticable and ingenuous, or did they hope against hope that they would be taken seriously by the governments who have taken it upon themselves to speak for the people who live within their territories? Has there been peace between nation and nation since those words were enscrolled? There have been some 125 wars since then. As these words are being written, there are more than thirty wars going on, maiming and killing warm-bodied men and women, and their children.

And millions more are being killed by starvation and the diseases starvation attracts, suffering which could be prevented if those swords could indeed be made into ploughshares. At no time have human beings needed so urgently to change history as now. But the prospect, alas, seems desperately bleak. These words are being written as a million children in Somalia are at risk from starvation caused by political power games and clan warfare,

and a thousand are dying every day; the children of the
breakaway areas of the former State of Yugoslavia are
being butchered by their old neighbours; and hundreds of
thousands of Kurdish children are being exposed to the
bitter privations of a winter in those inhospitable
mountains bordering Iraq, Iran and Turkey, all in the
cause of the adult pastime of defending national boundaries and accumulating power within them. These words,
then, must fall on incredulous eyes and minds which cannot imagine that Siddhartha Gautama's doctrine of
ahimsa, no violence towards any living creature, and
Jesus Christ's plea that we should love our neighbour,
would suddenly be heeded at the fag-end of a century
when war has been the most prominent human enterprise.

What is it that rejects the thought that war is not a
rational or civilised way of settling human problems?
Novelists, artists, composers of music, historians, poets
and journalists have tried for thousands of years to en-
noble wars and warriors. Valmiki, Kálidása, Homer, Virgil, all down the historical road to the composers of the
"Marseillaise", "God Save the King" and the American
National Anthem, have glorified war and military men.
Virgil began his *Aeneid* with *Arma virumque cano*. He
would "sing of arms and the man", meaning military
man. Almost all of these poets praised "their" side, the
"good" side, damned the "other" side, the "bad", and
called upon God, who was always "good", to bestow his
blessings on "their" side and damn the "ambitions" of the
enemy. Among the national anthems I know, only Rabin-
dranath Tagore's "Jana Gana Mana" celebrates the
brotherhood and sisterhood of people in the subcontinent
and does not demand the condemnation and extinction of
the "other". Very few British poets, Wilfred Owen is the

most outstanding among them, asked the poignant question, "Why?" Looking at the corpse of a soldier on the battlefield he asked: "Was it for this the clay grew tall?" But he wrote only a handful of poems and died young.

Yet, impossible as it seems, for the sake of children, war must be abolished. There is hardly a human being who will not agree with this proposition if you ask them. In the early fifties a small group of journalists, among them this writer, talked with Jean Paul Sartre about what he meant by existentialism. Without any preamble he asked: "Do you like war?" Each of us said "No." Sartre said, "Let us go to the street and ask the first hundred people we meet whether they like war. They will all say 'No.' I know. I have asked them. Talk to a thousand and they will all say 'No.' Talk to the first ten generals of the army, talk to a thousand military officers, and they will all say, 'No, they do not like war.' Yet there is war. That is existentialism."

Why, then, do we go to war? As I said in a previous chapter, governments go to war, not people. People have a vested interest in peace or, rather, not-war, even if they scrap with one another over land, over partners, over money, over ideas and, in some places, even over a neighbour's coconut. That vested interest is their children. Love for their children, at least for as long as they need parental protection, seems to be programmed into people's genetic inheritance. Governments resort to war because their relationships with other people's governments are determined by what they seek to protect: territory; ideology; cultural property which includes religion and language; and the power, wealth and status of the people in authority. War has also served many governments to rally popular fervour behind the rulers when they have become unpopular. Mrs Thatcher's Falklands

101

adventure was such a political exercise. Governments also need the preparation for war to benefit their supporters who make armaments. The reason was stated in those very terms by President Eisenhower who understood well the nature of war when he warned of the need to curb the activities of the "military-industrial complex".

Why do people permit their governments to make and buy arms costing billions which could be better used to give their children good education, good health, a good environment and a great future? And why do they raise such a patriotic storm when their governments become belligerent? The sixties generation achieved something remarkable. They exploded a three-thousand-year-old myth that it is sweet and proper, *dulce et decorum*, for young people to die for their country. They also made a dent in the ideologically inspired notion that there is something called a "Just War". The concept is dying but its traces cling to the memory, as the "virtuous" war against Saddam Hussein proved. But that war too had more to do with safeguarding American oil supplies from the Gulf than with the principle of sovereignty or, indeed, the defence of a democratic "New World-order" as the propaganda of the time tried to make out.

The United Nations General Assembly which passed the tediously negotiated Convention on the Rights of the Child committed itself to take separate and collaborative action to protect and restore children hurt by war. It pledged that it would "take all appropriate measures to promote physical and psychological recovery and social reintegration of a child victim of: any form of neglect, exploitation, or abuse; torture or any form of cruel, inhuman or degrading treatment or punishment; or armed conflicts. Such recovery and reintegration shall take place in an environment which fosters the health, self-respect and dignity of the child." Couched in the characteristic weasel-words of international diplomacy as these good intentions are, they provide a legal basis for taking action to mitigate the trauma suffered by children in war. The very use of the frigid words "the child", in preference to "children", is an indication of the tendency of politicians to relegate children to a remote place in their political and budgetary priorities. And one of the main defects of the Convention on the Rights of the Child is its failure to denounce war as one of the taproots of children's sufferings.

What we, members of the civil society who are serious about removing the "scourge of war" from human relationships and repairing the damage done to children's minds, need to do now is to keep these politicians' feet to the fire and demand that they take political action to allot the means to substantiate the Convention by adopting what Simone Weil pleaded for: a "Budget for the Eternal".

7

Education For Peace

Everyone I have talked to, and every writer I have read on the ill-effects of violence and war on children, seems to base their assertions against war on the profound assumption that peace is a fundamental human value and that aggression is an abnormal value for human beings. Contrary to the opinions of Konrad Lorenz (*On Aggression*) and the popularisers of his ideas like Desmond Morris (*The Naked Ape*) and Robert Ardrey (*African Genesis*), who assert that aggression is built into the genetic code of humans, and the people in the Reagan-Thatcher era who thought that people demanding peace were denizens of the lunatic fringe and so pejoratively dubbed "peaceniks", we who stand for non-violence prefer to believe with Richard Leakey (*Origins*) that it is cooperativeness which is our normal and natural inheritance, not aggression. With some wryness, which is also characteristic of Leakey's writing, they suggest that the stickleback fish, whose aggressive behaviour was one of the examples of Lorenz's dismal conclusions, is a little different from men and women, and that it is not aggression but cooperation which enabled us to make the transition from ape to man. With Leakey, some of us suggest that aggression began when we "settled down" to be farmers, and built fences around our properties against intrusion by our neighbours. Fences may make good surveyors' boundaries, but not necessarily good and peaceful neighbours because of the harsh imperatives of territoriality. As in the case of modern nations, "defence" of those fences is the justification for arming ourselves against attempts – imagined or actual – by our neighbours to violate the proprietary sanctity of our own piece of turf.

But, alas, everywhere around us, in international relations, within nations, within cities, in villages, in our nuclear and extended families and even between parents, and in the books we read – not just in pulp novels but in the "classics" of West and East, in the broadcast media and in all our histories, there is so much aggression and violence accepted as the norm in human affairs that it is easy to conclude that any hope of the abolition of war, the epitome of mass aggression, is nothing but a naive ideal which will never be possible for the human race to achieve. Yet, if anyone stops knee-jerking for a while and thinks about it, the assumption that it is not only possible, but necessary, "to learn war no more", to abolish war as a means of settling human conflicts and protecting children who are the embodiment of a human future, becomes clearly the only sane and secure basis for the very existence not only of human life but all life on Earth.

The capacity for destruction and extermination by non-nuclear war of the natural and human-made things which make up civilisation has been proved by the ecological as well as commercial results of the pyromaniacal sabotaging of the Kuwaiti oil wells following the Gulf War. A large-scale nuclear war, in contradistinction, would of course be the ultimate ecological disaster, not to mention its other catastrophic consequences. The decision of the Superpowers to reduce their nuclear armoury by fifty per cent has by no means reduced the threat of a nuclear war between nations. That threat continues. The possibility of a nuclear conflagration will exist even if the number of warheads is reduced to twenty-five or fifteen or five per cent. The ending of the Cold War certainly reduced the fear of Armageddon for the time being, but the threat of large-scale nuclear disaster continues to loom over the planet and its denizens.

It is significant that despite the thawing of the Cold War and the salutary reduction of tension levels in the international community, the sale of arms of ever-increasing sophistication has increased, not decreased. And it is significant that the five permanent members of the United Nations Security Council are the world's biggest arms manufacturers and merchants, despite the peace rhetoric they deliver in the Council and the lip service they offer to the ideals of the Founding Fathers of the United Nations. Abolishing the "scourge of war" from the world was one of those glowing ideals. Two statistics illustrate the extent of the hypocrisy and the irony of all this trafficking in death: eighty-five per cent of arms are produced by those guardians of peace and eighty-five per cent of their customers are Third World governments.

How can we, the people, who favour the elimination of the "scourge of war", dare to set our minds against these powerful forces which make the weapons of war and produce the geopolitical triggers which set wars ablaze? There may be logic in our plea but is there the rational force needed to give it substance and direction? From President Wilson to Prime Minister Olof Palme of Sweden and President Oscar Arias Sanchez of Costa Rica, leaders of nations have tried to negotiate the end of wars and the abolition of war as a lawful enterprise.

But arms budgets in many countries, particularly poor

countries, have doubled and tripled in the past couple of decades. In most of these countries, the "defence" build-up is not against the threat of foreign invasion but against the disaffection of their own people towards the government or the social class at the top of the economic pile. The same Third World governments which are vociferously demanding a larger share of the "peace dividend" they hope will accrue in the foreign-aid allocations since the stopping of the Cold War, are gleefully buying weapons in the international arms bazaar.

These extraordinary ironies have become too salient to be ignored, even in official public documents like the annual report of the United Nations Development Programme. Entitled "The Human Development Report", it monitors the ratio of expenditure, both development and military, and publishes the list each year. There is some grumbling about this by guilty nations who have seats or surrogate voices at the meeting of the Governing Council, but so far the authors of the report have not been intimidated.

This example is offered here as a clue to the only possible way to build a conflict-free Zone of Peace for children in the world of power. It is the pressure of the media, more especially the "alternative" media produced by development activists – people who are now calling themselves "civil society", whose "unofficial" voices have moved the minds behind the Human Development Report. And we know that in every progressive stand taken by the main-stream media it is the force of popular interest which has motivated them to change their ideas of what constitutes news. It was not the media which turned "environment" into a breakfast-table subject in the sixties but Rachel Carson's dire warning against poisoning nature with DDT, and the public outcry that followed.

The editors of *Time Magazine* were not primarily moved by holy thoughts at Christmas, 1989, to change the customary "Man of the Year" cover story in the first issue of the new year to "Planet of the Year". It was not a decision to abandon the old shibboleth that the American Press is not a bleeding-heart advocate of worthy causes. Decent and able journalists like Charles Alexander who saw the whole issue through from conception to production were personally committed to the environmental cause. But, by and large, it was the shrewd calculation that *Time* readers were putting at the top of their own personal agendas man's damage to the Earth and the urgent need to reverse that trend, which made it "professionally" right to honour the threatened planet on the cover of *Time*. The printed Press and the broadcast media adopted the environmental theme as a major concern only when President Bush and Margaret Thatcher turned green on realising that not to be seen and heard to be *for* protecting the environment was bad politics. And since the Press and television follow money and power as the lodestars of their news policies, the environment was deemed to be not just a "worthy" cause but a profitable theme to follow, day-in and day-out. The cumulative force of the voices of the powerless, joined through communications networks can move the mountains on which the powerful are enthroned.

The next subject of news attention may well be children who, like the environment, have neither vote nor voice in public policy-making, but have parents who have votes and can be empowered by civil society to speak and move through mass action motivated by knowledge and family interest in protecting the environment for the sake of their children. That amassing of civilian enthusiasm for the environment was the most important outcome of UNCED, the United Nations Conference on

Environment and Development, which drew some 40,000 people from around the world to Rio de Janeiro in the spring of 1992. This unprecedented gathering recognised that war is the most brutal threat to the environment: Chernobyl was still fresh in the memory and the oil-fires of Kuwait were still burning. The 7,000 "main-stream" journalists who were there concentrated not only on the fact that more than one hundred heads of state or government were present, but also on the conflicts of policy between both poor and rich countries and the "experts", who gave a fair imitation of contradictory expert court witnesses called by the prosecution and the defence to testify on the scientific "facts". The truth was plain to the "unofficial" human beings milling around Flamenco Park but it was obscured by the flurry of controversy in Rio Centro, forty miles away, where the official meeting was taking place. As a result, generally speaking, the news coverage missed the true significance of Rio: that the environment is the only binding ideology in the world, now that the Cold War is done. People in poor and rich countries alike are cutting across the barriers of race, caste and creed to embrace and protect Gaia, the Earth Goddess. As James Lovelock vividly expressed it, she is the mother of our children and therefore her health is our responsibility. And if the journalists and social scientists who went to Rio asked people why they were so passionate about the environment – as I did – they would have unhesitatingly said that their concern was action *now* to sustain the future. And, whether they were young or old, none had any doubt that the future lies in children.

Diverting Earth's bequests into war and violence against other human beings, and destroying the life-sustaining resources of the biosphere, are sure ways of depriving the children of the world of their legitimate inheritance. The most memorable poster on the walls in

Flamenco Park, where the ordinary people met in their
tens of thousands, expressed the sentiment simply and
tellingly: "We did not inherit the Earth from our
ancestors. We borrowed it from our grandchildren." But
trite as these sentiments have become, they serve to
ignite a different course of conscious thought about
people's relationships with others and with their environment. This, of course, is what education means. But it
means educating actual and putative parents. How shall
we connect this change of heart and mind, this metanoia
or repentance, as Jesus exhorted us to do if the world
were to be "saved", with the banishment of the "scourge
of war"? Should we not start with young children before
they become corrupted by the violent values of their
elders – which means you and me?

Unicef has gained some valuable experience in Lebanon where, in the heat of the bloody conflicts, a bold idea
was given its head in alliance with non-governmental
organisations which were running summer camps where
children and young people were given space to get away
from the daily horrors of their neighbourhoods. They
were young people from every faction embroiled in the
war. The Unicef Programme Officer, Anna Mansour, introduced a bright idea which made a difference: these
camps offered not only time and space for leisure but also
for learning about peace. Clarence Shubert, also of
Unicef, reported: "Nils Thedin came up with the idea of
'Children as a Zone of Peace'. Up to recently this concept
had been perceived from a physical point of view, protecting children physically in situations of armed conflict. In
Lebanon, a new dimension was added. Children should be
internally a Zone of Peace." This new dimension is what
gives the essential moral quality to Thedin's inspired
idea. Corridors and Zones of Peace which cut through

battle lines to protect children are admirable devices to take food and drugs to helpless victims of war, but as long as the war in human minds continues to be a motivating force behind warmaking, all attempts to eradicate the "scourge of war" from this Earth would be thwarted as we have observed since those words were placed on the United Nations Charter. Anna Mansour explained:

> Peace goes beyond ceasefire agreements among fighters. It builds on social justice, dignity and democracy. It is anchored in security felt in the body and the mind. It is based on self-confidence and trust in each other. It accepts human differences, whether sectarian, regional, social or political. It stems from respect for each other and the world we live in, particularly the environment.

Brave words. Good words. Unicef and their non-governmental organisation allies in the Lebanon programmed the ideas behind them and expected that within five years, three-quarters of the children of Lebanon would have experienced the process. The hoped-for "product" is that the next generation of Lebanese may become not only passive Zones of Peace but active agents of peace. Those who designed the Education for Peace Programme in the Lebanon as well as in Sri Lanka where too a brave handful of pioneers have launched themselves into a programme of peace education, knew well that peace, as they themselves say, "cannot be taught; it is a state of mind, and a way of life". Just imagine what they are attempting: trying to promote a peaceful way of being in children and youngsters caught in the babel of military discourse, in the rattle of indiscriminate bullets and the blast of bombs and grenades that have become the background

111

music of their lives. I doubt that even the tranquillised mind of an ascetic can easily remain still with such turbulence outside. But, despite that despairing thought, I must admire their conviction that a beginning has to be made. You cannot wait for peace to start developing a peaceful mind. And, perhaps, the best time to begin is in the midst of war when the need for peace becomes agonisingly real.

The objectives of these programmes may be easier said than done but their designs are clear:

1: to teach some techniques of peacemaking which *can* be taught, unlike peace itself; for instance, skills such as problem-solving and conflict resolution for themselves as well as others;

2: to increase children's self-confidence and self-esteem – the foundation of personal values;

3: to remove or warn against stereotypes of other cultures and ethnic groups;

4: to learn to analyse and detect prejudicial information projected by the media; and

5: to include peaceful universal values which are part of the human heritage.

I hope they will include parents and peers who are the nearest mainsprings of unfair prejudice, and the influences children must learn to evaluate before any of their ideas are taken in.

These goals are to be implemented through primary education: non-formal education such as drawing, sketching, painting, drama – street plays, for instance, or video vignettes produced and performed by young people involving their communities wherever possible. In the Lebanon experience, within a year of the start of the peace education programme, 125 peace camps, 300 day-care centres for younger children, 20 youth camps and 25 youth clubs were in operation to create Zones of Peace in the minds of children and young people. The experience of young people communicating their ideas to their younger children gave the programme enormous vitality and effectiveness.

In Sri Lanka, where the ethnic violence has not yet abated, and the prospect of a peaceful and durable solution to the civil war seems very dim at this moment, the worst danger to children, except to those living in the very centre of the storm who are constantly in mortal danger, is the increasingly pervasive notion that violence and war are the *only* means of solving the crisis. The peace-education promoters are hopeful that they will succeed in getting their programme into schools, both primary and secondary. But experience world-wide has shown over and over again that changing the school curriculum is one of the most difficult things to do. There is too much riding on maintaining the status quo: for instance, the convenience of the teachers who will not change, unless they are strongly moved by conviction or some other incentive such as the prospect of a promotion or a salary rise; the general reluctance to go against the stream even if people know that the stream is polluted by ignorance and prejudice, as happened in India recently when people who "should have known better" (as was repeatedly said) said nothing and did nothing when the fundamentalist Hindus raised the communal storm which destroyed the venerable Muslim mosque in Ayodhya; and, of course, the demand from parents that their children should not be distracted from their main purpose in school which is to equip themselves for employment.

These innovations are being studied and adopted elsewhere with Unicef's active encouragement. It all seems as futile as trying to stop a runaway train with a feather. But unless the effort is made, there is no hope whatever that war and violence will stop one day, some day, so that children will be able to grow to their natural capacity. The very thought that somebody has dared to make the attempt to prevent the pollution of militarism and terrorism from damaging the seedbeds of violence – the minds of children – is heartening.

But I feel it necessary to suggest here that those who are planning and managing peace-education programmes should ask themselves the question which Jiddu Krishnamurti would surely have interpolated at this very point: "Who is the teacher of peace and who is the pupil? Is the teacher of peace at peace?"

These interpolations may at first seem to be negative, obstructive and even irrelevant. But I suggest that they are fundamentally practical questions. They lead to other important questions as in all truly growing ideas which are all too often blocked by pat answers. Could "peace education" become an effective means of eliminating the "scourge of war" in the minds of children, if widely prevailing perceptions of education which regard children as empty sacks into which adult specialists would stuff gobbets of knowledge that they themselves have learnt, and doses of medicine into their bodies to keep them healthy, are to be the means by which this hopeful transformation of habitual and historically approved violence is to take place? How can peace and non-violence be taught by men and women who are not free from violence themselves? Is such a question misplaced in a reflection such as this on how to begin making the world safe for children?

It is certainly an awkward question, even an embarrassing question, which seems to set up what many will call a "merely philosophical" obstacle to earnest people and organisations who are panting to march into action and produce quantifiable results before their "mandates" or donor interest, or both, run out. The truth, alas, is that without "mere" philosophy, the results achieved are likely to be riddled with errors of understanding of how and why human beings behave in spite of being "educated" and "civilised". Remember, it was one of these highly "educated" and "civilised" nations of Europe which, just fifty years ago, perpetrated the Holocaust, one of the vilest acts of barbarism in history. For a more contemporary instance, just look at Yugoslavia and the process of "ethnic cleansing" – involving a war against babies – which is blazing away as these tremulous hopes for a world free of war are being enunciated. Without "philosophy" which offers moral insights into reality, we tend to emphasise ends at the expense of means. So we use violence to end violence and sow the seeds for further violence. Perhaps the most important lesson Mahatma Gandhi showed us by his work is that the dichotomy between ends and means is a false and dangerous division of reality. For him means *were* ends. The way we do things – however worthy our intentions – determines the quality of the results. The ends are means and, therefore, are *in* the means.

Such a monumental lesson from the most eminent exemplar of *ahimsa* or non-violence since Siddhartha Gautama is fundamental to any serious effort in peace education. And Krishnamurti's implicit injunction about the need for the teacher of peace to be peaceful within is also an essential pointer to the designing of any serious programme of peace education. All these great teachers and the sacral teachings of Jesus urge us to realise another important "fact" which has been borne out time and time again by experience and observation: generally, children are born in an ambience of love and peace. Unless their gestation period and time of conception has been made corrupt and turbulent by the actions of their parents, children "know" peace at birth. And if their infantile demands for warmth and food and tenderness – the familiar care they had received in the womb – is satisfied, they continue to know peace. Their natural ambience is peace. It is not necessary or possible to teach peace to infant children. It is very much like teaching grandmothers, or indeed grandfathers, to suck eggs.

Peace education, therefore, should begin with couples before they have children and include parents after they have had children. This, of course, is a very tall order especially in societies which have taken a mechanistic and institutional approach to child rearing, depending on crèche attendants, baby-sitting agencies, and kindergarten or pre-school teachers to look after their children while parents go about their own lives – working at some office, shopping or playing tennis or bridge. These upper-middle-class practices inevitably penetrate to families less well off and permeate the whole of society in varying degrees of intensity, depending on their income.

In rural societies where the ancient extended-family system still exists, despite the fact that the social fabric has been badly torn by urbanisation and "modernisation", the traditional lore is still passed on through songs and tales of nature which carry many connotations of peace and reconciliation of hurts between people, and between people and the natural environment they live in. Those glittering busy-bodies, the *devas* or angels, who look after children, always hang around trees and flower bushes, and send us rain are always welcomed as a blessing in a world of agrarian values. Those values "naturally" placed fertility at the top of the scale of social ethics, and art and literature were suffused by agrarian imagery. When the rather rare phenomenon of rain falling through sunshine occurs, in many rural societies, people's minds promptly fly to a piece of fertility folklore to explain it: to them it is a sign that there is a marriage taking place in the fox family living in the neighbouring scrubland. Agrarian values almost always harmonise and reconcile with nature in content and connotation.

The disappearance and breakdown of these rural societies and their peaceful values, which have been occurring at a breathless pace during the past half-century, have enabled other values of a harsher and more self-serving nature to replace them. Twenty years ago, seventy per cent of the world's population was rural. It seems likely that by the end of the century, seventy per cent of the people will live in urban and peri-urban areas. Their experience of the natural environment will be confined to urban-sized parks and potted plants, already being scaled down artificially to apartment proportions.

We need a Wordsworth of the cities. His work is still amply relevant to our contemporary world because though he was often called a "nature poet", implying that his main subject was the lakes and trees and leafy lanes, his main interest, like that of almost all poets, was the human being:

One impulse from a vernal wood

Can teach you more of man,
Of moral evil and of good
Than all the sages can.

Man, the human being, was the subject and the benef-
iciary of that arboreal impulse. If one could relate to the
natural environment respectfully, one would learn to respect oneself and one's neighbour. An urban environment
does not provide such value-impulses. The Trump Tower
in New York may raise emotions of awe and envy and
possibly deference to Mammon, but it cannot instil respect as does another recent prodigious architectural
achievement – the Baha'i temple in New Delhi. Stand in
the centre of the great chamber there and you will feel a
sense of profound stillness within yourself and outside.
That is respect. That is a profound educational experience of what peace is. The still place within is the
well of values we need to draw from if we are to abolish
the "scourge of war" for the sake of our children. We also
need a modern Charles Dickens to tell stories about the
plight of blighted children in our blighted cities. Isabel
Allende? Gabriel Garcia Márquez? Anita Desai? Where
are the novelists who are writing to our hearts and
wakening our minds to the horror of tens of millions of
young children who suckle off the urban streets in Africa,
Asia and Latin America, and the tens of millions who are
caught in the crossfire of civil wars across the world?

With all these thoughts affecting our minds, the
question remains: can peace and non-violence be taught
in the familiar ways that reading, writing and arithmetic
are being taught? The central need has been identified:
little children do not need to be stuffed with precepts and
knowledge about the value of non-violence and the importance of regarding the human race as one. They do

need to be protected from being influenced by their older siblings, their parents and their neighbours to adopt racialism and xenophobia as right and necessary stances in their relationships with others. This is where education is needed. The noble notion of peace education, I suggest, must begin with the community – with older children and parents – whose minds need to be cleansed of cumulative prejudices so that their inherent sense of belonging to the human community may be drawn out into their consciousness where the pollution of violence has imprinted its smudges.

The experience of the Education For Peace Programme in the Lebanon in the past five years, where parents and older children participate in the process, bears this out. And what about teachers? Searching for minds free of violence would be an impossible thing. But since one of the best attributes of wisdom is being willing to accept second-best, perhaps the best we can do is to select teachers who are willing to prod themselves into conscious recognition that they themselves are not free of the violence put into their minds when they were children and who are prepared to share their predicament with their pupils. Peace education would then become participatory communication, a mutual search for liberation from violence rather than a "subject" one teaches the other. It would then be a redemptive process of mutually reinforcing absolution. The result might well be a deep understanding and appreciation of peace which applies not only to the absence of war but peace in our own daily lives.

8
Children and the Nation State

In the spring of 1992, an extraordinary gathering took place in Addis Ababa. It was not one of those laboriously concocted conferences of African nation states held under the banner of the Organisation of African Unity, but five presidents from the Horn of Africa and East Africa attended. It was not a conference of United Nations agencies, but Jan Eliasson, the newly appointed chief of the United Nations office responsible for humanitarian affairs, and senior representatives of the High Commission for Refugees, the World Food Programme, the United Nations Development Programme, the World Health Organisation and Unicef attended. The heads of government, including Omar Hassan Ahmed al-Bashir of Sudan, held private sessions before the main conference and went home. They left their advisers, spokesmen and other surrogates behind. The leaders of the Sudanese rebel movement were also there before, during and after the main conference. John Garang, the charismatic leader of the rebellion for many years, did not come. He was dealing with a serious schism in his movement and was intensely preoccupied with resisting the southward thrust of al-Bashir's army which was trying to dig in forward before the rains bogged down its heavy equipment in runnels of mud.

The conference had been convened by Abdul Mohammed, a young Ethiopian intellectual-cum-activist who is Director of the Inter-Africa Group based in Addis Ababa and who has earned a widespread reputation in Africa and the West for his thoughtful and sustained critique of the nation state as a suitable unit for organising human affairs – such as looking after children – and managing the planet's resources. Remarkably, Mohammed has also earned a solid reputation among some of the most fiercely suspicious African nationalists of Africa, like Daniel arap Moi of Kenya and Omar Hassan Ahmed al-Bashir of the Sudan, for being totally trustworthy and discreet with their innermost thoughts which they share with him. Abdul Mohammed has no grand titles, no retinue of minions to do his bidding, no pompous "presence", and no money. He has something else though: a priceless commodity called sincerity. It is not a measurable quality but it is palpable and obvious in his refusal to carry tales between contending parties, or to confuse tactics and strategies, the common mistake of the traditional diplomat who wins plaudits for his or her adroitness but never for trustworthiness. Mohammed's diplomatic forte is the exact opposite of Henry Kissinger's. He never resorts to using "leverage", the smart euphemism for using bargaining chips, whether they are territories, aspirations for power, or the security and survival of groups of human beings. He has no such chips to play with. He is good at listening to people. With a score of people waiting to talk to him, he seems to have all the time and attention the person with him seems to need. He breaks in occasionally with a comment and very soon you realise that he is a moderator, in the pre-seminar use of the word, using only common sense rather than cerebral force to move his interlocutor into the sensible centre of a strident dispute. When an African leader asked him: "But what have we got except our sovereignty?" Mohammed appreciated the force behind the argument, a sensibility which evidently showed on his face. Then he replied: "But what is that sovereignty being used for? You are not being invaded from outside. You are sheltering behind your sovereignty to fight a war against your own people." There was no accusatory tone or impertinence in that remark. It was just a statement of fact which made its mark without wounding the self-esteem of a head of government. The discussion then went on naturally to the need to reduce the intensity of the violence so that peace negotiations could take place in a less passionate atmosphere and so that the sufferings of children, who are the future of Africa, would be lessened. The practical outcome of that conversation was the re-affirmation of the need for Zones of Peace for children.

This was the most remarkable thing about that Addis Ababa conference. So many powerful people, most of them utterly embroiled in a civil war as was al-Bashir, or in an election frenzy as was arap Moi, or in desperate efforts to maintain order in and the territorial integrity of the country amidst renewed rumblings of dissidence from peripheral areas as was the new President of Ethiopia at that very moment, took time off to come to Addis to discuss and overtly or tacitly, by their words and presence, to reaffirm the principle of Zones of Peace for the benefit of children and other non-combatant victims of war. At the general conference almost every speaker, including the insurgent leaders, dwelt on the theme of Corridors of Tranquillity, Zones of Peace or Zones of

Tranquillity for the sake of these innocents. It was interesting to note that United Nations agency heads and the International Red Cross too were speaking the language of peace which Unicef had adopted in its efforts in El Salvador and Uganda to make a reality of Nils Thedin's dream of "children as a Zone of Peace".

There was absolutely none of the usual turf consciousness which usually frays the edges of inter-agency relationships, and the Unicef representatives who participated wisely refrained from asserting their copyright over the terms being used. Nils Thedin's words, in varied forms of usage, had now become a part of the jargon of the international community and it was best to let it develop organically. People adopt new language when they need it for their own purposes. That is how a newly coined word or phrase becomes currency.

In the corridors, the journalists hovering about were displaying their customary scepticism about the prospects of peace or even of a reduction in the level of intensity of the civil war in the Sudan. The newspeople who had covered the affray for years were certain that al-Bashir had gone home in a hurry to drive his troops farther into the heartland of the rebellion and to secure new ground before the rains came. They believed that he was determined to exploit the open friction between John Garang and his associates and that the time was unpropitious for any serious peacemaking efforts by the United Nations or by any individual like Abdul Mohammed, however persuasive he might be as a moderator. In the event they proved to be right. The weather is a powerful determinant of the course of and opportunism offered by war, as generals from the time of the Trojan Wars to the present day have found. The army redoubled its efforts to capture large tracts of land in the southern sector and the rebels, now divided and at a disadvantage against the heavy armoury of the government, gave ground, moving northward in scattered formations to wait for the rains to come to their aid.

Nevertheless, the need for the Corridors of Peace continued. It was now apparently universally recognised that the obligation of a sovereign government to allow the intrusion of the international community to succour the innocent victims of war seemed to prevail over the "right" of a nation state to preserve the inviolability of its national boundaries. To be sure, the Zones or Corridors of Peace were there by the express permission of the government, but they were there. They were sanctified by the human obligation to see that the human needs of survival were provided for the most vulnerable groups among the non-belligerents in the population.

As do most of us who have worked with Unicef, Abdul Mohammed understands well that Zones or Corridors of Peace are but temporary expedients designed for a specific purpose: to provide a channel through which food, essential drugs, vaccines and equipment for maternal and child health care may be carried to people embroiled in war, people – particularly young children – whose lives have been shattered by the violent erasing of their life-lines, frail as they might have been. These corridors, being short-term means of alleviating suffering and providing some sort of promise of survival for children, cannot easily be extended to cover other life-enhancing needs such as education. Indeed, with considerable diligence and purposiveness, education for peace camps were provided in the Lebanon during the worst of the fighting.

In the early eighties, Jim Grant, then leading the UN effort to prevent what many believed would be a massive famine in Kampuchea, decided to build his rescue and re-habilitation actions around community schools. It turned out to be a happy idea because the schools became not just spaces where some rudimentary pedagogy was available, but also facilities for community gatherings and discussions between ordinary people and the field workers of aid missions. This was one of the earliest instances of active participation of people in their own rehabilitation and development. Desirable as it seems for an education element to be tied to Zones or Corridors of Peace, there is a serious risk to it because both sides of a war have a cause or ideology to purvey (remember the attempt by the Americans in Vietnam to "win the hearts and minds" of the Vietnamese?) and "education" is always suspect by both sides as a vehicle for carrying insidious enemy propaganda.

The temporary and inescapably hurried nature of Zones or Corridors of Peace – Operation Lifeline Sudan, certainly at its inception, was no more than a piece of inspired ad-hocracy – entails many weaknesses: the Zones are just soup-kitchens and dispensaries constructed on a movable landscape; they are inadequate when measured by any standards except what it takes to survive the day or, at most, week; and they are often charged with being cost-ineffective, as though a child's life can be entered in a ledger.

What is most significant in the decade of experience of corridor-making, intense and varied as it has been, is that it is a humanitarian concept which has touched a core of human value deep in the consciousness even of men who have been raised and trained in a military culture. Napoléon Duarte and his guerrilla opponents, Milton Obote, Okello and Museveni in Uganda, al-Bashir in the Sudan, have each been trained to win wars without compunction, but they have all been stirred in that deep place within them which responds to the call of children.

It is this feeling of primal obligation which has caused
people in the past ten years to open a window in their for-
tified walls of sovereignty to let in the humanitarian lifeblood needed to keep children alive while their elders try
to settle their power quarrels by killing one another.

Is it too fanciful to extrapolate from this experience the
thought that these Corridors and Zones of Peace for children may be the wedge that was needed and will eventually serve to separate human beings from war? The
sceptical promptings of memory and the calculations of
realism suggest that, perhaps, it is. Such doubts are the
bitter fruit of history which has tilled the skulls and
bones of millions of human beings killed in war into the
soil. The Italian Foreign Minister, Gianni de Michelis,
expressed the positive view at the UN General Assembly:

> . . . the right to intervene for humanitarian ends and
> the protection of human rights is gaining ground.
> This type of intervention [he was clearly referring to
> Corridors of Tranquillity] has become an *idée-force*,
> and the most truly innovative concept of the remain-
> ing decade of this century . . . Intervention that is
> primarily aimed at securing protection of human
> rights and respect for peaceful co-existence is a pre-
> rogative of the international community, which
> must have the power to suspend sovereignty when-
> ever it is exercised in a criminal manner.

Perhaps de Michelis spoke too bluntly even if he was
lauding an *idée-force*. There was alarm immediately in
the camps of many countries in the non-aligned group
who have not enjoyed their sovereignty long enough to be
willing to yield any of it for whatever purpose. Also the
notion of coercion made them bristle. Many of them, even

those who had supported President George Bush's coalition war against Iraq because Saddam had infringed
Kuwait's sovereignty, were concerned that the second
agenda of the United States – to topple Saddam Hussein
from his seat – might be repeated elsewhere, even in
their own countries. They would not oppose the idea of
humanitarian corridors, and would actually welcome
help to protect the vulnerable groups, but *only* with the
willing agreement of the governments in office. Not by
coercion. Their spokesman told the General Assembly:

> Our worry stems out of history, when many of us
> as colonial subjects had no rights. The respect for
> sovereignty which the UN system enjoins is not an
> idle stipulation which can be rejected outright in the
> name of noble gestures. And an essential attribute
> of sovereignty is the principle of consent, one of the
> cornerstones in the democratic ideal itself. And to
> our group it involves partners, mediations and, in
> our global context, a fantastic convergence of the
> burning desire to help, and the wonderful sense of
> relief in freely and willingly receiving the help. The
> UN cannot and must not be commandeered into
> forming an assistance brigade that will deliver its
> gifts by coercion. That will definitely be unaccept-
> able to us.

Such arguments may seem spurious and self-serving to
the critics of the concept of nation statism. Yet they cannot be easily discarded and replaced by the flimsy hope
offered by the rediscovery of that inner core of conscien-
tiousness hidden in our sense of obligations to our children. It is that very same centre of being that has been so
demonstrably touched by the red-alert signs about the

desecration of the environment. It was this globe-wide realisation that we human beings have fouled our nests so thoughtlessly and dangerously which brought thousands of alarmed men and women to Rio de Janeiro in the summer of 1992, to talk over what needs doing to repair the damage and restore the Earth to a state of sustainable health.

But armament manufacture and sales are still mounting. Despite all the talk of disarmament and peace dividends, the arms bill exceeds one trillion dollars. To repeat, some eighty-five per cent of those arms are bought by Third World governments. In most cases this expenditure is to defend their own regimes and the economic interests of their friends. But in public they justify it on the plea that they need to defend the "sovereign borders" of their nation states against foreign threats to the integrity of those borders. This last point demands our attention now since we are reflecting here about the possible effectiveness of the widening of humanitarian Zones of Peace as a means of avoiding war for our children's sake. This was the second most important item on Abdul Mohammed's agenda at the conference in Addis Ababa: the military culture that nation statism breeds and the impact of war on the lives of the people, especially the least able to find a foothold on life, when their context is being constantly and drastically changed by the vagaries of war.

It is important to perceive the difference between the nation state and "nationalism". Hans Kohn who lived in the United States – which had wisely chosen the federal form of unity-in-diversity 200 years ago and paid the bill 100 years later in a devastating civil war (virtue is often more expensive than vice) – observed in the 1940s that: "Nationalism is first and foremost a state of mind, an act of consciousness." Nationalities, he lamented, "defy exact definition". We cannot find their sources but, expressing themselves through their special rites, beliefs, value systems and languages, they came into existence a long time ago.

Basil Davidson, the distinguished British historian to whose latest book *The Black Man's Burden* I owe these quotations from Kohn, carries on the thought:

> And with this gift of separate tongues each to be developed into a supremacy and made 'more real' by ejecting as impure words borrowed from abroad . . . the nationalities become ever more divisive. So the trouble starts. As Hans Kohn concludes, this is when "nationalism demands the nation state". Then this "creation of the nation state strengthens nationalism". And the gas chambers loom ahead.

Davidson's environment impels him towards the metaphor of the gas-chamber. Mine, being Sri Lankan, leads me to the metaphor of the Hindu priest being roasted alive and Tamil children being hacked and flung in the dirt when Sinhalese language chauvinism was first stirred by Prime Minister Solomon Bandaranaike in the late fifties.

It may have been difficult, as Hans Kohn found, to define or even describe nationalism in the forties when the world was carved up into empires and spheres of influence. Now, fifty years later, some 120 new nation states have sprung from the debris of a crumbling imperialism. And since the unity of many of those states is already being eroded and their value impugned by internal struggles for identity among the subnational groups which had been subsumed by the larger entity ruled by a central government, it is now possible to scrabble in the dirt and attempt a recognisable description – if not a definition – of what nationalism seems to mean to people. It is a sense of being one people with a shared history, shared customs and lifeways, a common language and a shared basket of values which includes religious and spiritual teachings and practices. This complex of relationships gives people the meanings which they crave to understand and to accept, with varying degrees of conviction and doubt, the multitude of events, processes and changing circumstances which affect their lives. This sense of being one with a nation may and does exist irrespective of where one lives and what travel document one carries.

The Jewish experience during the diaspora and even after the establishment of the State of Israel provides an excellent example of the ubiquity of "nationalism". A Jew does not have to be a believer in Judaism or an inhabitant of the nation state of Israel to be and feel as a member of the "Jewish Nation". Similarly, the insistence of many indigenous groups in North America on referring to themselves as the "Onondaga Nation" or the "Hopi Nation" is evidence that their sense of nationalism is distinct from their common ownership of the lands which they once lived in and cared for. The ironical truth is that many of the stoutest "patriots" whose declamations of national fervour one hears around the world are those who will never return to the countries of their birth.

This inner sense of nationalism is reflected in outward behaviour in people's food preferences, in their choice of partners for themselves or their children and in the religious rituals they practice on family occasions such as births, marriages and deaths. Perhaps the most deep-rooted of these usages is language. People, except those who have been completely colonised in their minds, have an abiding love affair with the language in which they read their first words and learnt their first numbers. Words are not merely the coinage of communication: to say "pass the salt" or for air traffic controllers to give instructions to pilots taking off and landing. Words are symbols which contain the most profound values of our inner lives. They are the dark repositories of our dreams. People will defend their language vociferously and violently. It is not perchance that the first rumblings of centrifugalism in India occurred when Prime Minister Jawaharlal Nehru, in his desire to make progress in building a unified nation state as successor to the British Raj, proposed that Hindi be adopted as the official national language of India. Tamil Nadu was the first state to protest and there were dissident demonstrations in Kerala, Maharashtra, the Punjab, Assam and many other states. In the mid-fifties Prime Minister Solomon Bandaranaike of Sri Lanka, in his haste to attain power, expediently promised the majority Sinhalese electorate that he would make "Sinhala only" the national language of the island "within twenty-four hours". That was the first major breakpoint with the Tamil minority, a wound which festered for forty years and has now turned gangrenous. Canada has been going through its own language ordeal with Quebec whose French-speaking majority has tried more than once to break away as a separate state, much as the Tamil Tigers have been demanding in the North of Sri Lanka.

These are the nationalisms which come to the surface when macro nation states are formed out of a congeries of micro "nations". The process takes time as it has done in the former Soviet Union, in Yugoslavia and in India, but it appears that it cannot be stopped. The only choice is between willingly loosening the iron bonds which have held it together and letting it happen peaceably and without undue disruption and refusing to see its inevitability – even its advantages – or letting it degenerate into a dirty cat-and-dog fight and eventually into a racist civil war. It is wise to suppose that the next stage of this process of political evolution might well be confederations of micro nationalisms. When these subnationalisms break away they may not take long to realise that, isolated in this intricately enmeshed world, they are economically and politically unviable and that the only sensible thing to do is to seek a confederal relationship with their neighbours.

An instructive and, as it later turned out to be, an ironic story was going the rounds in Moscow shortly after Mikhail Gorbachev's first meeting with Prime Minister Margaret Thatcher. Intrigued by her comment: "We can do business with this man," curious political observers dug into the substance of their conversation and found that much of their time together had been spent on discussing a question Gorbachev asked her at the start: "How did you British transform your Empire into a Commonwealth?" That was when she was certain that the dissolution of the Russian Empire was uppermost in his mind. She reminded him that the process of decolonisation had taken fifty years and was not yet complete. Gorbachev did not have fifty years. The empire he inherited had long outstayed its span of life and was so rotten that it had to crumble in a hurry rather than dissolve peacefully. The irony is that Boris Yeltsin stole the concept of Commonwealth from Gorbachev and took the credit for it. He will have to pay a price for it because the crumbling will go on for many years, and the centripetal confederal impulse will not be evident until the breakdown stage has been completed.

The centrifugal pulls of micro nationalisms seem to be

accelerating in many areas of the world. Their direction is masked by the counterbalancing force of regionalism which is the first difficult stage up from the monolithic nation state and towards confederalism and, eventually, the ideal of "One World". Some of these countries are experiencing ethnic and religious centrifugalism within their boundaries, but have tried to hold them down by force and promises of a first-class citizenship and freedom of worship to the minorities. They may yet avoid the worst effects of violent centrifugalism by leap-frogging over to the next stage of true confederalism among their neighbours. Indeed this has been suggested as the only possible solution for the ethnic conflicts in Sri Lanka and Ulster. In a confederation of South Asia, the Tamil minority of Sri Lanka need no longer fear that their language and ancient culture will be overwhelmed by the chauvinism of the Sinhalese majority. There are sixty million Tamils living across the Palk Straits in Tamil Nadu.

The nation state is dying but it is dying hard. Why is it still a formidable force in people's minds? Most people, it seems, assume that the nation state, as we know it, has existed ever since the human race began. It takes a jolting realisation to understand that the modern nation state is not much older than our century. Germany was not Germany until Bismarck forged a nation state out of the multitude of petty principalities where German was spoken. Italy was not Italy until Count Cavour and Victor Emmanuel II of Savoy cobbled a nation state together. India was not India until the British put their steel umbrella over the subcontinent and called it the Raj. Even little Sri Lanka had two and three kingdoms at the same time at various periods of history. They all disappeared and the entire country became Ceylon when the

British established their imperial writ throughout the island. All sorts of symbols such as the crown, the sceptre, the flag, the anthem, and war systems for loyalty to the governors of the new political entity were introduced to sell people the concept of the nation state. Nationalism has been around a long time in human history. The nation state is a nineteenth-century construct, essentially a European device for corralling diverse nationalisms under a single flag, signifying a greater unity and strength for all than people in separate groups had previously enjoyed.

Actually, the nationalist movements which led to decolonisation after World War Two were progressive forces which unified people of many subnationalisms to fight for the common cause of independence. At that time its meaning was simple: get those white people out. Basil Davidson again offers an apt quotation from Jacques Rabenemanjara of Malagasy, writing in 1958: "One thing's certain: in today's political vocabulary the word nationalism means, generally, the movement of coloured peoples against Western domination. What does it matter if the word doesn't really describe the phenomenon to which we all like to apply it?" The leaders of the independent movements in Asia and Africa who dreamed of "self-rule" in an independent land-mass, big or small, were mesmerised with the notion that, when free, they would adopt the political and economic practices, the territories, social values, legal systems and all the rituals of governance which they would inherit from the departing colonial powers. The rhetoric of "nation building" which every independent leader from Nehru to Nkrumah to Sukarno were spouting at that time meant that they too would persuade, coax, cajole, threaten, intimidate, do violence on, and make power deals with, every powerless minority to keep them from asserting their own independence and establishing their own small "nation states".

To be fair, they meant well. Most of them have been so profoundly imbued with and impressed by the material achievements of the European nation states within less then one century of their formation – even the former Soviet Union had managed to transform itself from a backward agrarian country into the second most powerful state in the world within half a century of nation statehood – that it seemed to them that there was no better model to follow. India abandoned the Gandhian ideals of non-violence and self-government by half a million village republics and concentrated power at the centre as Socialist planning requires. Sukarno played the interests of the *ulemas*, the Socialists, the Nationalists represented by the army, and the Communists against one another in a loosely constructed central Nasakom (Nationalists, Socialists, Communists) Cabinet under his direct control in his paternalistic efforts to build a nation state, succeeding in making one of the most richly endowed countries in the world into one of the poorest.

One generation of children lost their life opportunities in the process, being forced to live off the nationalist slogans of the government. African inheritors were even keener to abandon their own heritage, believing the colonial propaganda that "tribalism" was a primitive form of social organisation, and they began to play the nation-state game with gusto. The whole process was hastened by mobilising popular reactions to real and imagined threats to the national borders. One, and in some instances, two generations of children's prospects of growing to their full potential have been sacrificed to the political power struggles of the élites entrusted to manage the nation state. And when the superficial unity which prevailed at the start wears thin and the minorities begin to assert their claims to fair shares of power, it is the children who suffer most, their entire lives being blighted by years of communal conflict and civil war.

Abdul Mohammed and other critics of the nation state know well that it creates rather than solves problems – indeed that it *is* one of the root problems which causes famine in one area when there is abundance in another, and that it causes environmental damage because acid rain and toxic substances are no respecters of national boundaries. But there is no way to stop them from spreading unless there is common action across the borders. They also know well that their criticisms of the nation states, however cogent and rational, will be taken as utopian at best and quixotically aberrant at worst.

I share Mohammed's views about the nation state but prefer not to argue the case against it on logical grounds. It is not a subject that lends itself to rational debate. There is a legitimate emotional case to be made against it. The "patriotism" it engenders and the chauvinistic zealotry of micro nationalisms which inhabit the same borders, lead almost certainly to conflict, civil war and, not infrequently, to international war. The principal victims of war are children, the future of the human race. Children lose their life opportunities, even the meagre life opportunities of the poorest. They lose years of schooling, they lose their health and become stunted in body and mind because of early malnutrition brought by disease and lack of fresh and sufficient food, and they lose their young green lives. That, I believe, is what touches even the flintiest hearts which have been hardened by the military culture. "Children as a Zone of Peace," Nils Thedin's dream, may be the idea which will eventually cut across the bombast and the calculations of the arms manufacturers and the warmakers.